Chase Greatness

Life Lessons Revealed Through Sports

Frank Agin

Author of
Foundational Networking
Building Know, Like and Trust
To Create A Lifetime Of Extraordinary Succes

CATHY,
BE GREAT!

Chase Greatness

Life Lessons Revealed Through Sports

Frank Agin

Copyright © 2014 by Frank Agin. All rights reserved.

Printed in the United States of America

Permission to reproduce or transmit in any form or by any means, electronic or mechanical, including photocopying and recording, or by an information storage and retrieval system, must be obtained by writing to the author, Frank Agin. He may be contacted at the following address:

Post Office Box 30724, Columbus, Ohio 43230
Toll free: (888) 267-7474 • Email: frankagin@amspirit.com

Ordering Information:
To order additional copies, contact your local bookstore.
Quantity discounts are through the author.

ISBN: 978-0-9823332-6-6

Published by:

418 PRESS
A Division of Four Eighteen Enterprises LLC
Post Office Box 30724
Columbus, Ohio 43230-0724

Interior design: Hilary Jones
Cover Design: Kim Mettille of
LogoTizeGraphicArtStudio.com

For Linda Sue

My O-Dark 30 Training Partner,
Home Team Co-Captain, and
Family MVP

[Pat], [Pat], [Pat]!

Ready... Break

Contents

High Fives & Chest Bumps 1

Chapter 1
Prelude To Greatness 5
  There Is Greatness. Just Look.

Chapter 2
The Game Of Change 9
  Don't Let Anything Stand In The Way Of You Going After Your Dreams.

Chapter 3
The Arsenal 13
  Look Around. There Is Someone To Lift Up With An Encouraging Word.

Chapter 4
Team Chemistry 17
  Keep Your Team Intact. Greatness Will Follow.

Chapter 5
A Lesson From The Heartland 19
  Opportunities To Exhibit Compassion Do Not Find You; Rather, You Find Them.

Chapter 6
Six Kicks In The Summer 23
  Wherever You Serve Others, You Serve To Lift Yourself.

Chapter 7
Great Scott! 29
  Mediocrity Has Always Railed Against Greatness. Endeavor To Be Great Anyway.

Chapter 8
The Octuple Co-Championship 31
  Focus Less On Being Number One, And More On Just Being Great.

Chapter 9
A Pitchless Win 35
  Some Achievements Are Hard Fought, Others Not. However, All Are Earned.

Chapter 10
Life Is A Decathlon — 39
Success Is A Function Of Trying To Do Consistently Well At Everything.

Chapter 11
An Awesome Kick — 43
You Have Wonderful Talents. Use Them Where You Can Add Value.

Chapter 12
Fourth And 15 Years — 47
You Are Never Too Far Down To Mount A Comeback.

Chapter 13
McNasty — 51
Your Talent Is Important, But Not More Important Than Your Character.

Chapter 14
Still The Best Policy — 55
Nothing Can Beat The Honest Person.

Chapter 15
Do You Believe In Miracles? — 61
Success In Life Is Driven By Things Other Than Miracles.

Chapter 16
Unstoppable — 65
The Only Limitation You Really Have, Are The Ones You Impose On Yourself.

Chapter 17
In The Face Of Tradition — 67
Follow Your Heart And Passionately Do What You Want To Do.

Chapter 18
Four Eighteen — 71
Set Worthwhile Goals, But Keep Going Once You Achieve Them.

Chapter 19
The Wizard Of Westwood — 75
Work Hard. Success Can Be Yours. Just Not Tomorrow.

Chapter 20
Shoeless Ron Hunter   79
You Have Influence. However Big Or Small, Use It For Good.

Chapter 21
Stand Tall   81
You Are Great In Your Own Right. Bow Before No Earthly King.

Chapter 22
Eleven Seconds To Courage   83
Life Will Give You Tragedies And Setbacks. Forge Ahead Despite Then.

Chapter 23
Standing O-H ... I-O   87
Great People Applaud The Achievements Of Others.

Chapter 24
Singles Score Runs Too   91
Seemingly Inconsequential Opportunities Are As Important As Great Ones.

Chapter 25
Bonnie Richardson High   95
Sometimes, It's Just Up To You.

Chapter 26
A Perfect Shame   97
Don't Live By Others' Recognition Of Your Achievements.

Chapter 27
The Fiesta Fake Out   103
Work Hard And Sacrifice; Someone Will Notice.

Chapter 28
One For Dad   107
Little Things In Your Hands, Can Be Immense In The Hands Of Another.

Chapter 29
Harvard Beats Yale 29-29   113
Don't Buy Into The Hype Of Others.

Chapter 30
Responsible Winning　　　　　　　　119
Be Of The Same Character In Victory, As In Defeat.

Chapter 31
Heroic Assistance　　　　　　　　123
A Loss Is Only A Loss. It Is Not Failure.

Chapter 32
Winning By Taking Second　　　　　　　　127
Do The Right Thing, No Matter The Cost. You Win In The End.

Chapter 33
Find Your Greatness　　　　　　　　129
Know That In Every Victory And In Every Defeat, You Have Achieved Something.

Chapter 34
The 3:59.4 Lesson　　　　　　　　133
What Matters Most Is What You Believe To Be Your Abilities.

Chapter 35
Hanging On By A Finger　　　　　　　　135
Life Will Throw Difficult Choices At You. Get Used To It.

Chapter 36
A Perfect Mistake　　　　　　　　139
Always Be Open To Contrition And Forgiveness.

Chapter 37
The "Around The World" Walk-On　　　　　　　　145
It Is Never Too Late To Embark On Something New.

Chapter 38
The Slowest Runner In America　　　　　　　　147
You Don't Have To Be The Best. You Just Need To Try Your Best.

Chapter 39
The Rookie Back-Up　　　　　　　　149
To Do The Things You Want, Sometimes You Have To Do The Things You Don't.

Chapter 40
What's In A Name   153
There Is Great Value In Knowing The Names Of Others.

Chapter 41
The Drought   155
Whatever The Circumstance, Keep After It. Eventually, You Will Break Through.

Chapter 42
We Are One   159
In The Grand Scheme Of Life, We Should Stand Together.

Chapter 43
Greatness Continues   163
Look Around You. Greatness Is There To Find.

About The Author   165

Box Scores & Statistics   169

High Fives & Chest Bumps

"You are publishing a book! Really? WOW!" I hear this from time to time. While the adulation is flattering, part of me wants to respond, "No, we are publishing a book." Trust me, any book is a collective effort.

In the case of *Chase Greatness*, it started with Lewis Howes (*LinkedWorking* co-author and kindred entrepreneurial spirit) encouraging me to share some of my collection of stories on his SportsNetworker website. From there, I realized that I did have enough to form into a meaningful book.

After that, I consulted with Reputation Group's John Millen (my sometime mentor; sometime protégé) as to the tone and direction I should take. John has the ability to tell me what I really need to hear (and it is not always glowing), but he can do it in a way that we remain friends.

Then much of what is on these pages came from countless others who graciously and eagerly shared articles, leads to stories, and website links. This included high school and college teammates. There were business acquaintances with whom I mentioned this book in passing. There were even childhood friends with whom I reconnected via the wonder of Facebook.

With notes and outlines in hand, the writing begins. Certainly writing a book can be a lot of work. I estimate that it takes me on average about an hour per page to get that first draft done. Some words just seem to roll on to the screen. Every word that comes to mind is perfect and they all fit together perfectly.

Then, some pages appear on the screen painfully slow. My mind cannot quite find the words and when it does, my fingers cannot seem to find the right place on the keyboard. It seems that more than any other, I am hitting the "Backspace" key. Then it seems, after I have cleared out my mistakes and I am ready to move on, the words have escaped me.

Whatever the case, eventually I have written the entire book. While it sounds impressive, it is not. A book is nothing more than letters molded into words ... words crafted into sentences ... sentences built up to make paragraphs and chapters. In reality, this is the easy part. Trust me, you could do it as well.

Once I have the first draft written, the book is really only half done. Here starts the painstaking chore of smoothing over what is truly a rough draft ... trying to make sense of sentence structure ... questioning word choices ... seeking out and correcting my every typo. This started with my recent trio of interns (Stephanie Donavan, Hilary Jones, and Charlie DeHart) and then moved on to a litany of other reviewers and proof-readers (which amongst others included David Hess, Dave Smith, Amber Flack, and my wife, Linda).

Then we need to layout the interior. Armed with a wonderful InDesign template developed by Wendy Hollinger (Phoenix Graphics), AmSpirit Business Connections intern Hilary Jones endured just "one more change" over and over and over again to get the layout just right ... for now, anyway ... I think.

Although literary types proclaim, "you should not judge a book by its cover," that does not stop an author from pouring his or her soul into its every detail. This was no different. Thanks to all who contributed pictures ...

> Debbie Burke (fellow parent at St. Francis DeSales High School);
>
> Becky DeLozier (fellow parent at St. Francis DeSales High School);
>
> Amy Flowers (fellow GNA Futbol Club Board Member);
>
> Lewis Howes (*LinkedWorking* co-author);
>
> Patty Huhta (fellow Houghton High alum);
>
> Sue Johnson (fellow Houghton High alum);
>
> Mary Lombardo-Graves (No. Illinois University professor and favorite cousin);

Sammi Schmidt, Esq. (Minnesota attorney and wonderful niece);

David Smith (AmSpirit Business Connections member and friend);

Kelley VanLanen (fellow Houghton High alum and Facebook friend); and,

David Wieging (fellow St. Matthew Athletic Association Board Member and friend).

With pictures in hand and a general idea as to the concept, the talented Kim Mettille (with LogoTizeGraphicArtStudio.com) whipped this all into the wonderful cover art you now see. Of course, she is patient as well, having to return volley on my seemingly constant changes and tweaks.

Beyond the writing, editing, and overall book production, I want to extend some appreciation to my three kids. If not for them, I would not still be – after over half a century of life – so engaged in athletics and enchanted by sports. Whenever I hit my knees, I cannot help but thank God that Lucas lost interest in chess, Logan bailed on dance, and Chase never got into scouting.

In summary, publishing a book is a collective effort. That said, on this one, I had a great team. So, high fives and chest bumps to all those I have mentioned (and to those I missed, for whatever reason, a heartfelt apology).

Chapter 1
Prelude To Greatness

There Is Greatness. Just Look.

Sports are great. It seems that for many of us, we wrap our lives in it. Almost every day there is something related to sports, whether we are playing, watching, or talking about it. Can you imagine a life without sports?

Sports occupy us. You likely spent countless hours on weekends, after school, and during recess in pickup games where you divvied up teams, creating unconventional strategies and plays that you gave silly names. You also might have been alone – just you, a ball, and a goal or hoop – working on that move or shot, dreaming it was for the win in the final seconds of the championship game. Even today, you might find yourself preparing for that race, beer-league game, or fitness challenge.

Sports entertain us. You spend evenings or afternoons braving the elements in the stands, at the rink or on the field, diamond, or pitch just to watch your favorite team or player, even if it's only your own kid. You plan holiday celebrations around game time or perhaps suspend household rules (no food outside the kitchen) for the occasion. Then you spend hours at the sports bar cheering, high-fiving, and hugging complete strangers who, for the game, are kindred spirits.

Sports mark the passage of time. You remember it was three days before your ninth birthday when you hit that first home run in little league. You remember exactly that 10-year playoff drought, as it occurred during your 20's. Or, you remember your friend's anniversary better than your own because he got married on the day your team upset the number one team in the country.

As much as sports serve to mark time or engage and amuse you, often within it there are messages – messages that provide compelling lessons about life. Society tends to lump these under one general heading of sportsmanship. If, however, you really examine these with an open mind, you can see that what happened is something that transcends athletic competition.

Over the course of a season, within a single game, or even within a single moment involving a contest you get the opportunity to witness humanity at its best. These are moments of great compassion or courage. These are wonderful acts of honesty or determination. These are times of incredible discovery about what you too can be. These instances are many, many things.

The important point is that all of these moments – no matter where they occur or who they involve – have application to your everyday life, if you let them. They can serve to inspire you to be something more than you are. More forgiving. More contrite. More humble. More accepting. More determined. More ... More ... More ... The list could go on and on.

In November 1983, I was fortunate enough to be part of one of these moments. Inspiring and uplifting, that event motivated me to look for similar events. What I have come to realize is that these stories do not happen every day. Moreover, they do not occur in every contest. Nevertheless, they are all around us, and they have been happening for years.

Over the last 30 years, I have been sort of a collector of these tales (made much easier with the advent of the Internet). In that time, I have kept a sort of file of these, adding more and more as I learned of them. From time to time, I would delve into my growing collection of moving and encouraging stories as a means of fueling my own perseverance.

Last year, I took a moment to sort through my collection. Being my anal self, I began to categorize and catalog the stories. There were dozens with diverse messages and lessons. It was at this moment that I realized I wanted to share – somehow – this assortment of inspiration. From that epiphany, the idea for this book was born.

Read on. Read this from cover to cover. Or simply page through and pick and choose the stories that "speak loudest" to you. However you decide to digest this collection of entertaining sports stories that offer life lessons, I encourage you to examine your own conscience. In so doing, look for inspiration and motivation to be more than who you are and more of what you can be. In short, use this book to *Chase Greatness*.

Chapter 2
The Game Of Change

Don't Let Anything Stand In The Way Of You Going After Your Dreams.

The United States is a wonderful country. This nation has freedoms unlike most any other nation. It has, however, some shameful aspects to its history – one of those being its treatment of minorities.

For centuries, this nation (even before it was a country) engaged in the practice of kidnapping and enslaving people from the African continent. Through the leadership of President Abraham Lincoln and the courage of many others, the 1863 Emancipation Proclamation eradicated slavery and freed millions of people suffering under it. With one executive order, the United States made an enormous move towards racial equality.

As gigantic as the Emancipation Proclamation was, it did not create absolute racial equality. For decades, individual states established and continued the practice of creating laws and policies that served to treat those once enslaved in a much less favorable way than white Americans. Individual state laws segregated schools, provided separate restroom facilities, and even required separate seating for people known over time as colored, black or African American.

The United States government then took another giant step towards racial equality in 1964. On July 2, 1964, Congress passed and President Johnson signed into law the Civil Rights Act, outlawing major forms of racial discrimination (as well as ethic, religious, and gender discrimination).

A democratic government, by its nature, does not act of its own free will. Rather the government takes action because those who elected it require such action. As a result, in drafting, modifying and passing the Civil Rights Act, the United States government acted in response to the will of the people.

While the undercurrents for this civil rights legislation were likely present for decades, it began to formalize and build momentum in 1955. That year, several prominent African Americans (best known being Malcolm X and Martin Luther King, Jr.) began a campaign to highlight the inequities faced by African Americans in this country, as well as set about to demand change.

American history refers to this as the civil rights movement. This movement inspired change through several means. There was civil resistance and nonviolent protest. Leaders of the civil rights movement also conducted sit-ins and boycotts. Furthermore, they organized marches in demonstration of the cause. In 1963, however, the civil rights movement received some unintended assistance from a basketball team in the heart of the Deep South.

Located in Starkville, Mississippi, Mississippi State University (MSU) was a basketball power from 1959 through 1963. At that time, it was on par with other Southeastern Conference (SEC) basketball powers such as Kentucky and Florida.

Through this basketball prowess, the Bulldogs won the SEC basketball title four out of five years. As a result, the NCAA gave the Bulldogs an invitation to participate in the 1959, 1961, and 1962 national championship tournament. In each of those years, however, MSU declined that invitation.

This refusal to participate had nothing to do with economics – the financing of travel, feeding and housing of a team for an extended period on the road. It had nothing to do with academic performance – the concern over the well-being of the student athlete. This was merely about race – the state of Mississippi had an unwritten rule for college basketball teams: "Don't play against teams featuring black players."

Though unwritten, MSU had strictly adhered to the rule. In 1963, however, the Bulldogs had clinched their third straight SEC title. The players, coaches, and University wanted to test themselves beyond the conference play. In short, they had a dream. MSU wanted to win the national title.

To accomplish that, they would have to accept the NCAA's invitation to play in the national championship tournament. This meant, however, that they would risk violating the Mississippi rule and play against teams that had African American players.

MSU elected to take the risk. That risk, however, became more likely once the NCAA released its 25-team tournament seeding. MSU had a first-round bye in the Mideast Region, but it would likely play in the second round against Loyola University – Chicago, a team that started four African-Americans.

When the Loyola Ramblers destroyed its first round opponent, Tennessee Tech, 111-45, the risk became reality. Immediately, state government officials within the state of Mississippi moved to convince the MSU basketball team to forfeit the Loyola game, upholding the prohibition against playing teams that "featured black players."

The MSU players and coaching staff, however, were determined to go for their dream. They defied requests to forfeit (including one from Mississippi Governor Ross Barnett) and proceeded with plans to travel to East Lansing, Michigan for the Mideast Regional tournament. Before the Governor could serve an injunction preventing the team from traveling, Coach Babe McCarthy and his Bulldog players flew out of the state under the cloak of darkness.

Even once they were safely out of state, there were those who continued to pressure the MSU team not to play. The Ku Klux Klan and other racist individuals sent letters stating, "You better not play!" and, "Your life is in jeopardy." The Bulldogs remained undeterred. They were pursuing a dream.

Even Loyola players were the target of threats and pressure. They also received correspondence from the Klan as well as warnings and threats from African American groups. While these groups aimed to terrorize the Ramblers into not playing, they had a dream as well.

In the end, however, neither MSU nor Loyola would succumb to intimidation. They were determined to play. They each wanted to be national champions.

On March 15, 1963, at Michigan State University's Jenison Fieldhouse, MSU's Stan Brinker and Loyola's Vic Rouse shook hands before the opening tip of the semi-finals of the Mideast Regional tournament. While they represented different races and came from different worlds, that night the one thing they had in common brought them together. They each had a dream of winning the national championship and nothing was going to stop them from trying to achieve it.

What do you really want to achieve? You might have a personal goal, such as running a marathon, writing a novel, or building your dream home. You might have a professional aspiration, such as meeting a sales quota, earning a promotion, or starting a business.

What might be standing in your way from making a run at achieving it? There is no doubt something. Success is never easy. Often, others are competing with you for the same thing. At times, by the very nature of the achievement, it may take you months, years, or even decades to accomplish it. Or it might be that there are long-standing social stigmas that serves to thwart your efforts. No matter what you look to achieve, intervening forces and circumstances will challenge you, as success is never easy.

Whatever the case, do not let these apparent obstacles stop you. Even if it delays your achievement, find a way around the complications. Even if it takes more effort to achieve it, work to climb over those obstructions. Moreover, even if you have to, gear up to power through those barriers. Do not let anything deter you from trying to achieve what you want to achieve.

Chapter 3
The Arsenal

Look Around. There Is Someone To Lift Up With An Encouraging Word.

Through their childhood, my kids were involved in travel soccer. These are teams comprised of boys and girls with an interest in playing soccer on a serious level as well as have acumen for doing so. One of the team my kids played for was known as the Gahanna Futbol Club Arsenal. The various teams of the Arsenal traveled around the central Ohio area playing travel teams in their appropriate age group from other local communities.

The first year my oldest son, Lucas was involved with the Arsenal, he decided that he wanted to share the duties of playing goalie with another boy on the team. Although they each had the opportunity to play other positions during the game, for one-half of each game my son would play goalie while the other boy would take on these responsibilities during the other half.

Like any young boy or girl participating in youth sports, Lucas has had good days and he has had bad ones. However, there was one particular match in first year during the season-ending tournament that things became terrible.

The team that the Arsenal was playing this particular match was simply a better team. Their boys were bigger and faster, more physical and more skilled than our boys. Although the Arsenal did all it could to keep pace with this other team, it was only a matter of time before our boys would wear down. While the half started with the Arsenal only down 2-1, midway through the second half the Arsenal yielded to superior size and skill.

As it turned out, the coach slotted Lucas to play goalie during the second half of the match. This was not a particularly good time to be in goal, however. The opposition peppered Lucas with shots and forced him to defend a string of breakaways.

Although he, like the rest of the team, made a valiant effort, in the end he gave up five goals. After the first two goals, my then 8-year-old son was dejected. Goal three, four and five sunk him toward being devastated.

After the teams shook hands, I met up with Lucas on the field. He stopped and looked at me with his little long face. I got down on a knee to hug him and as I did, he started to cry. We just stayed there for what seemed like a couple minutes. Although different in some respects, it was a moment that all parents endure with their kids at some point or another. You want to take the pain away, but you just do not know how.

Then out of nowhere, Lucas' coach, John Grimme, came over and knelt down beside us. He patted my son on the back and reassured him that he had played a good game. He went on to share with Lucas that three or four of the goals were not his fault. He explained that long before the other team got their shots, his teammates had a half dozen other breakdowns along the way. He shared with Lucas how his older son, who was also a goalie, had been put in the same predicament just a few days before.

As for the shot or two that Lucas should have stopped, Coach Grimme gave him some quick advice as to what Lucas should do next time. Most importantly, he simply reminded Lucas to use those goals as a learning experience.

At that point, Lucas did not stand up and walk away dry-eyed and smiling. However, the reassurance and encouragement provided by his coach helped him stare down a setback. That afternoon, in the next game, Lucas was back in goal with a confident swagger as if the morning debacle never occurred.

Look around you. Someone is having a bad day. For whatever reason, things are not going well for them.

You might not be able to alter the situation or circumstances that have put them in a funk. You, however, can alter how they feel about themselves with a few words of support and encouragement. This simple act can have a profound impact and may even positively alter the course of someone's life.

Knowing this, you should be ever ready with an *arsenal* of things that you can use to help others who is having a bad day, whether it is in sports, business, or life in general. You can remind them that better days are ahead. You can also remind them that whatever setback they are experiencing is likely not fatal or even long-term for that matter. You could even remind them that everyone has these times in their life and that tomorrow is another day.

Wherever and however, find that person who is down and infuse some encouragement into their life.

Chapter 4
Team Chemistry

Keep Your Team Intact. Greatness Will Follow.

B ack in 2002, an article appeared in the *Academy of Management Journal* that addressed the importance of team chemistry in professional sports. In their research, the three authors were trying to determine just how successful professional sports teams were in their efforts to tinker with the composition of their teams. After all, it seems that professional sports teams are continually trying to create the perfect concoction of stars and role players in their never-ending quest for Super Bowl rings, World Series titles or Lord Stanley's Cup.

In the study, Shawn L. Berman (Santa Clara University) Jonathan Down (Oregon State University) and Charles Hill (University of Washington) compared the records of 23 National Basketball Association (NBA) teams from 1980 to 1994. They hoped to determine just how successful these NBA teams were at improving themselves by altering the team composition through drafting, trading, and free agent acquisitions.

What the authors focused on was "shared experience" on each team. They measured a team's shared experience, by looking at both its members' overall tenure on the team and their actual on-court minutes with other players. In other words, they attempted to determine just how consistent a team's roster and on-court line-up was from one year to the next. And more importantly, what impact did this consistency have on the overall success of the team.

Adjusting for other factors that affect performance (such as player quality and age), they found that teams with less turnover tended to improve their win-loss records significantly from one year to the next. These results were not due simply to the tendency of winning teams to keep their lineups intact. In fact, player stability also gave a big boost to losing teams, which presumably had little incentive to stay with the old rosters.

Teams with losing seasons in one year won an average of 5.7 more games in the following year if their level of shared experience rose. At the same time, if a team shuffled their roster, similarly situated teams only won 1.2 more games the next season. In short, team chemistry is very important and teams that stay together tend to play a lot better together.

Similarly, your life is comprised of lots of teams. You have a family team, which includes a spouse, siblings, and other relatives. You have a personal team, which includes friends and acquaintances. You have a community team, which includes neighbors, place of worship, civic organizations, and government entities. You have a professional team, which includes employers, employees, colleagues, clients, and vendors.

While you rely on these team members to help you achieve success, none of them are perfect. There are conflicts, shortcomings, and other frustrations. As such, from time to time you may have the inclination to trade out one teammate for another.

Whatever the reason, resist the temptation. At the very least, carefully think about the situation before you decide to displace one relationship for another. Rather than committing energy to somehow replacing certain aspects of your team, use that effort to re-tool those once-valued relationships through new focus and greater commitment. You may find that with just a little bit of work, you can help the team function more effectively – thus turning losses into wins.

Chapter 5
A Lesson From The Heartland

Opportunities To Exhibit Compassion Do Not Find You; Rather, You Find Them.

In December 2003, Brandon Teel attended Kearney Senior High School and was an unassuming wrestler for the high school team. As a senior, he was a backup in the 189-pound weight class for the Bearcats, the No. 2-ranked team in Nebraska.

One day, the Bearcat wrestling coaches approached Brandon with an unusual request. It all started when the head wrestling coach for the Lincoln East Spartans, a nearby rival high school and No. 1-ranked team in the state, e-mailed Brandon's coach. In the e-mail, the Lincoln East coach asked his counterparts at Kearney if one of their wrestlers would compete in a junior varsity match against one of the Spartan wrestlers.

The request was unusual because the Spartan wrestler was a freshman named Trevor Howe. This Lincoln East freshman had Down Syndrome, a chromosomal disorder resulting in mental retardation and an inability to fully develop motor skills. Thus, for Trevor wrestling was a struggle.

The Kearney coaches agreed to find someone to wrestle the East Lincoln High freshman. They knew that it was going to take a special kid for this situation, so they quickly decided to ask Brandon Teel to take on this challenge.

However, the challenge was not in winning the match. Under normal circumstances, an experienced senior would be too much for a freshman. Moreover, under these special circumstances, Trevor did not stand a chance against Brandon.

The challenge was in the stipulations placed on the match. The coaches asked Brandon not to pin Trevor for two periods. They also asked the Bearcat senior not to hurt his freshman opponent. The

Lincoln East coaches just wanted Brandon to let Trevor experience wrestling in a competitive match.

Brandon accepted his role. Additionally, Brandon further agreed that he would not pin Trevor at any point during the match. Rather, Brandon would allow the match to proceed for a full six minutes and he would beat Trevor on points.

For a young competitive athlete at a wrestling powerhouse like Kearney Senior High School, Brandon's agreement to allow Trevor to remain competitive was noble in and of itself. If the story were to stop there, it still would be worth telling. However, it did not end there.

Once the wrestling match began, something happened to the Kearney Bearcat senior. Brandon Teel was overcome with what can be described as a tremendous wave of class, generosity, and compassion. Picking the appropriate time, Brandon allowed himself to be pinned, giving the victory to the freshman.

"He was really working – he was trying so hard," Brandon told Craig Sesker, a sportswriter for the *Omaha World-Herald*. "I was supposed to win on points in the third period, but I didn't think it would be right for me to beat him. It ended up being better this way anyway."

When the referee declared victory for Trevor, the entire gymnasium erupted. Trevor jumped up and down. He hugged his coach. He hugged his dad. Both wrestlers received a standing ovation. Brandon received accolades for his sportsmanship.

On Saturday, December 13, 2003, 17-year-old Brandon Teel gave Trevor Howe something he might not otherwise have had – the thrill of a lifetime to step onto a wrestling mat and earn a victory. He gave Trevor's parents something that they might never have expected. He gave all those in attendance a wonderful experience – the sheer joy of one person's unlikely triumph. And Brandon Teel gave us all a lesson.

The lesson is that moments of great compassion and generosity do not find us. Rather, we find them. Brandon did not have to lose. He did not have to allow himself to be pinned. He could have done exactly what the coaches had agreed – give Trevor a hard fought experience, not hurt him and take the victory in the third period – and no one would have thought less of him. Rather, Brandon chose a nobler course. He saw an opportunity to give to another and he took it.

More importantly, consider this: Brandon Teel was just a kid. He was just a 17-year-old kid, competing in a high school wrestling match. It was just a junior varsity wrestling match, somewhere in small-town Nebraska. There was nothing extraordinary about this situation, yet Brandon found an opportunity to express wonderful compassion.

Given this, and considering your own relatively successful circumstances, it should be easy for you to find an opportunity to make your own expression of compassion. Look around you. There are those who are disadvantaged or in need somehow, some way. Find that opportunity to exhibit your great compassion and act on it.

Chapter 6
Six Kicks In The Summer

*Wherever You Serve Others, You
Serve To Lift Yourself.*

Technically, the scoreboard read "4th Down and 1 Yard To Go." In reality, it was only six inches. As the Hematites were only on their own 19-yard-line, normally they would have played it safe – punt the ball away and rely on a staunch defense. Today, however, they had come too far to play it safe.

In coming too far, it was more than the nine-and-three-quarter yards they had gained in the previous three downs. It was more than their four post-season wins or even their one-loss regular season record. It was more than holding a 20-14 lead with four minutes left in the game against a heavily favored Detroit Loyola team. It was more than the eight-hour drive from the shores of Lake Superior to Detroit's Ford Field for the 2012 Michigan High School Athletic Association (MHSAA) Division 7 state championship.

In coming too far, it had nothing to do with down and distance, wins and losses, or highway miles. It was about psyche. In the past two years, the 6,500-person mining town of Ishpeming, Michigan had endured more than their allotment of tragedy, pain, and sorrow. In 2010, the football team was in this exact position – playing in the state championship game. Unfortunately, they were on the losing end of a 28-26 contest to Hudson High School.

Certainly, a state championship loss is far from tragic. That penultimate position is the envy of every other team but for the champions themselves. It was this loss, however, that seemed to set in motion a cascade of tragedy.

In 2011, Derrick Briones, the star receiver on the state runner-up team, died unexpectedly. The loss left the community numb. It, however, was especially hard on the football players, who were for the first time having to confront the death of a school friend and teammate.

Derrick's death seemed to affect Daniel Olson the hardest. Daniel was the son of Ishpeming's football coach and the star quarterback on the 2010 state runner-up team. Complicating the death of his teammate, Daniel felt a deep responsibility for the title game loss.

These events seemed to conspire against him. He was suffering from severe depression and anxiety. Although, he sought professional help and tried making a fresh start at Division III St. Norbert College, the mental illness consumed him.

On July 19, 2012, Coach Jeff Olson found his lifeless son's body in their home. He had taken his own life. The Ishpeming football program reeled again.

Time moves on, however. After a couple weeks of mourning, football began. While things might never be the same for the players and coaches, being on the field offered a temporary relief from the pain and sorrow. The worst seemed to be over. The season started and the winning began. With winning, there was some semblance of healing.

Tragedy, however, was not done with this Michigan town. Seven games into the season, on October 5, 2012, Christopher "Bubba" Croley died in an automobile accident. He was riding in a car with his family as they traveled south towards Wisconsin. A drunk driver in a pick-up truck went left of center on Highway 141. He hit the Croley family's Chevy Impala head on. Bubba died enroute to the hospital, the day before his 14th birthday.

While Bubba was not officially part of the Hematite football family, he was a highly regarded eighth grader in its football system. Moreover, Ishpeming is a small town. Anyone is likely only a connection or two away from knowing everyone. Thus, the team knew Bubba well enough that his tragic death opened fresh wounds. It seemed as if the pain and suffering would never end.

Despite all this tragedy, pain, and sorrow, there seemed to develop a heightened sense of community. Families rallied around families. Players were supportive of their coach. Classmates bonded like never before. This was most evident as it related to one special player, Eric Dompierre.

Eric had been born with Down Syndrome. This rare chromosomal disorder affects cognitive function, motor skills, and physical development. Despite this, he was on the football team and the backup kicker, described as "fun and funny with plenty of friends" and "known for keeping the team loose."

Over the previous two years, however, Eric and his family were in a battle of their own. Following the school's recommendation, Eric's family held him back when he was in elementary school. It was the right decision, but it was a decision that had latent consequences.

Under MHSAA rules, a student is not permitted to compete in high school athletics if they reached their 19th birthday prior to September 1st of their senior year. When Eric, who was involved with football since the fifth grade, was a freshman, his parents knew this rule would affect him.

Starting his sophomore year, the family petitioned administrators for a waiver. When the MHSAA denied the family's request for an exception to the rule, they did not accept that result. Neither did the community.

Amidst all the tragedy, pain, and sorrow, the community rallied support for Eric as he and his family endured quasi-government bureaucracy up close. Players testified and wrote letters of support on their teammate's behalf. The community conducted its own campaign.

Eric never got an exception to the rule. Rather, through his efforts and the efforts of the community behind him, the entire rule was changed. After meetings, committees, and proposals, the MHSAA put the matter to a vote. Representatives of 94% of Michigan high schools decided that students with disabilities could play sports even though they had reached the age of 19 by September 1st of their senior year.

The caring support did not stop there, however. While all Eric wanted was a chance to be an official member of the football team his senior year, he got more. Coach Olson, still dealing with his own very tragic and personal loss, named Eric as their starting extra point kicker.

Moreover, Coach Olson stuck by this decision, even after Eric missed his first point-after attempts in their opening game. And he stuck with that decision when Eric missed a second time. And after the third. As well as the fourth and then the fifth.

In fact, the entire team rallied around this decision. Inspired, they drove for touchdown after touchdown in an effort to give Eric one more chance. This was about something more than winning. For Coach Olson and the team, it was about giving someone else the sheer joy of accomplishment.

In the end, on his sixth attempt, Eric split the uprights. He recorded his first official extra point. He enjoyed the adoration and celebration of family, fans, and teammates as if he had just won the state championship game.

The state championship game, however, is the tail end of this story. With a little over four minutes left and facing fourth down and six inches, the Hematites were not about to punt the ball. In more ways than almost any other team could imagine, they had come too far. Even though they were only holding a six-point lead with the football on their own 19-yard line, the coach and the team with the support of the community chose to go for it.

The team from Detroit Loyola, however, did not stand a chance. At that moment, whether it was six inches or six yards, Ishpeming simply would not allow themselves to be stopped. They were avenging a loss two years earlier as well as uniquely hardened by three horrible tragedies. Moreover, at the same time the wonderfully caring they had for each other inspired them.

After two attempts to draw Loyola offside, the Ishpeming quarterback took a quick snap from center and plunged forward behind his center. Securing the first down, the Hematites were able to run out the clock and claim the state championship they failed to achieve two years earlier.

Tragedy, pain, and sorrow are part of life. Unfortunately, we will all endure them at one point or another. Loss of loved ones. Enduring illness. Extended personal setback. In these times, it is easy to feel sorry for yourself. It is easy to become cynical and self-centered. These feelings are almost natural inclinations.

Fight these tendencies, however. Rise above them and do not forget to care for those around you. Whatever your circumstances and however you might feel, if you contribute to those around you – through kind words and selfless actions – life has a wonderful way of balancing itself. Thus, by serving others, even though you might not feel that you have the strength, you will essentially serve to lift yourself.

Chapter 7
Great Scott!

Mediocrity Has Always Railed Against Greatness. Endeavor To Be Great Anyway.

In the summer of 2008, nine-year-old Jericho Scott was just your average kid growing up in New Haven, Connecticut. No doubt, he was enjoying time around home playing with friends, and trying not to get too hot.

That summer what he really wanted were three things. First, he wanted to play little league baseball – after all he enjoys the game. Second, he wanted to be on a team with his friends – after all, that is half the fun. Finally, he wanted to be a pitcher – after all, he was good at it.

The Youth Baseball League of New Haven proclaimed that it wanted kids to be happy and have fun in their program. Despite this, league officials told young Scott he could not have all he wanted. In essence, they told him that he could only have two of the things he wanted. Under no circumstances, however, could he have all three.

You see, Jericho Scott was somewhat of a pitching protégé. His fastballs soared to home plate at 40 miles per hour, which was remarkable for a nine-year-old. Moreover, his pitches were not wild and he never hit anyone. In fact, he was consistently accurate, finding the strike zone time after time. In a word, he was a great pitcher.

Given that, parents of opposing teams lobbied league officials to ban Scott from pitching for his undefeated, championship-bound team. Their kids could not hit his pitches and they were fearful of the effect of that humiliation. Given that, Scott could be on the team with his friends. He could be a batter. He could play any other position. They just did not want him pitching in the 8-to-10 age division.

The league concurred. They informed Scott's coach that he could no longer pitch on that team in that age division.

Scott and his teammates, however, would not accept that decision. After playing one game in another position, Scott was determined to play the position he loved – pitcher. The next game, however, when he took the mound, the opposing team forfeited that game. They simply packed up their equipment and left.

In the end, the league took action. It effectively disbanded Scott's team and awarded the league championship to the second place team. Through the influence of parents, the league granted average players an advantage over a great one.

This, however, is not limited to a small baseball league in Connecticut, as it is typical of many instances in life. Through history, unfortunately, people of mediocre ability and subpar work ethic have stood against the talented and hardworking. They have used peer pressure to discourage the effort of the tireless, diligent, and meticulous. Moreover, they have used the system to undermine or limit the abilities of the talented. Using whatever means they could, they have railed against greatness.

Despite this, never be afraid to continue to work hard and be resilient in your efforts. Make every effort to seize all opportunities to exercise your talents, whatever they may be. In short, endeavor to be great no matter what anyone says or does.

Chapter 8
The Octuple Co-Championship

Focus Less On Being Number One, And More On Just Being Great.

A few times a year in every state in most every conceivable high school sport, the sanctioning body for high school athletics ranks, seeds, and pairs team for the state tournament. These pairings then square off. It is "win or go home", as the teams whittle themselves down.

In the end, only one team (likely in each division) has an unblemished record in tournament play. At this point, polls don't matter. The thoughts of armchair quarterback, point guards, and pitchers everywhere become irrelevant. This team is the number one team in the state, at least until the next season begins.

The State Championship is something about which many teams can only dream. For others, they have a reasonable hope, although the odds are still long. For a few schools in certain sports, if they achieve anything less they deem the season a failure.

In 2008, it was unclear as to which category the final two hockey teams fell in the Michigan High School Athletic Association Division I State Championship. On March 8th, Marquette High School and St. Mary Preparatory School were each one victory away from claiming the title.

These two schools were very different in many ways. The St. Mary Eaglets were from a private Catholic high school and the Marquette Redmen were part of a public school system. St. Mary Preparatory High School was located in Orchard Lake Village about 35 miles from the championship game site, the Compuware Sports Arena, near Detroit.. The Redmen hailed from Marquette, Michigan, located on the shores of Lake Superior in Michigan's Upper Peninsula, about 200 miles due north of Green Bay, Wisconsin and 450 miles from Detroit.

Orchard Lake Village is a relatively affluent suburb of Detroit, with executives and upper management from various facets of the auto industry. The Marquette area is more or less a working class community, with an economy supported by higher education, mining, and tourism.

While the two schools were very different, they were familiar with one another. In 2007, they squared off in the state championship as well, with St. Mary defeating Marquette 4-2. This rematch, however, was not necessarily inevitable. St. Mary, the two-time defending state champions, ended the regular season with barely a .500 record, but both teams started to play their best hockey as the post season began.

Most high school state championship games tell a story. Whether that story is an epic battle, an underdog rising up, or superior team asserting its will, there is a story. The St. Mary-Marquette state championship game, however, had a very different story to tell.

Through the first period and a half, there were plenty of scoring opportunities. Defensive heroics and great goaltending, however, were preventing any goal production. Nine minutes into the second period, that changed. Marquette's Mike Peterson scored, allowing the Redmen to take a 1-0 lead going into the final period.

In the third period, there was again lots of back and forth, but nothing to show for the effort. Peterson's goal appeared to be enough as the teams played deep into the third period. With just a few minutes left, St. Mary's coach called a time out and used the opportunity to execute an age-old hockey strategy: He pulled their goalie out of the game and added a sixth attacker.

The strategy worked. With 1:32 left in regulation, St. Mary's Tim Hooker scored a goal. Shortly thereafter, time expired with a 1-1 tie. At this point, the story of the St. Mary-Marquette hockey championship began.

After 45 minutes of regulation hockey, the teams faced off for sudden-death play. In the first eight-minute overtime period, much like the first half of regulation there were a lot of action. The teams were desperate to get or prevent the game winner. As hard as the Redmen and Eaglets fought, however, neither could tally that decisive score.

This back-n-forth, edge-of-your-seat action continued on into the second overtime. And the third. And the fourth. And the fifth.

The extended game continued. The players from each team were becoming increasingly exhausted. Coaches and trainers worked to keep their players hydrated.

The game moved through a scoreless sixth overtime. Parents got involved. They scrambled to get their sons oranges, bananas and other sustenance. After a seventh scoreless overtime, one coach's wife brought to the players an armload of Nutter Butter cookies purchased from the concession stand to the players.

At the end of the eighth scoreless overtime, the teams were busily preparing to play a ninth. Before they could, however, the Michigan High School Athletic Association stepped in and did something profound. After 109 minutes of heated action and four hours, 15 minutes after it started, they called the game. In so doing, they crowned the Orchard Lake St. Mary Eaglets and Marquette Redmen co-state champions.

While there was debate in the media and amongst high school hockey fans as to whether the MHSAA should have ended the game in a tie, it did. The high school sports governing body cited the fact that they were endangering the health of the student-athletes and that they came to close too running over into Sunday (which its rules prohibited).

Some questioned as to why the MHSAA did not do something else to determine a champion – a coin toss, a shoot-out, something. The reality is that nothing was in the rules to allow it. Thus, doing anything would be unfair.

Whether or not the MHSAA official result on the St. Mary-Marquette game was appropriate is something that others can debate. Certainly, the declaring of the co-champions did not definitively answer the question as to "Who's No. 1?" It was, however, in the best interest of the student-athletes.

Nevertheless, in pronouncing an octuple co-champion, the MHSAA still did something important. It served to celebrate two great teams.

Far too often in life, you can get caught up wasting needless energy trying to prove or proclaim yourself (or someone) as the best, biggest, or whatever superlative we can interject. This may relate to your business, career, sales performance, customer service abilities, or ability to maintain a green lawn.

In reality, it would be near impossible to make a definitive determination on any of this. And even if you could, it would have very little long lasting value. Thus, wouldn't you be better served devoting that effort to being great at what you do (or at a minimum, the best you can be)?

In so doing, you are resolving that you share a co-championship with one or more others. While this might not officially deem you as being number or the best, it serves to celebrate your greatness.

Chapter 9
A Pitchless Win

Some Achievements Are Hard Fought, Others Not. However, All Are Earned.

On July 7, 2009, the Colorado Rockies were tied 4-4 with the visiting Nationals in the top of the eighth. With two Washington batters already down and one on first base, the Rockies were intent on not falling behind. Their plan was simple: Secure one more out, get the lead in the bottom of the eighth, and hold on for the win.

It was time for strategy. Rockies' managers called to the bullpen, seeking the best match-up for the Nationals player heading to the batter's box – Nyjer Morgan. A few moments later the pitching coaches sent to the mound a veteran relief pitcher, Alan Embree.

Other than four games in his inaugural season with the Indians, Embree was a relief pitcher. His role on the team was simple: Come into the game at some point for a tiring starting pitcher. From there, somehow he was to keep the team in position for a win, whether that meant holding onto the lead or holding ground so the offense could stage a comeback or go ahead.

The left-handed reliever took the mound. He immediately began to deliver some warm-up pitches to his catcher and in short order he was ready to pitch. He adjusted his hat and glove one last time, placed his foot on the rubber, and took a deep breath to gather himself.

As Embree was preparing to enter his wind-up, anticipation built amongst the Colorado fans at Coors Field. They hoped that their team's strategy would pay off. The Washington Nationals, however, had a strategy of their own.

While the Nationals were committed to the batter at the plate, they hoped to change the situation. Washington manager Manny Acta gave the sign. He directed Austin Kearn – who was on first after hitting a single – to take a sizable lead off. Kearns was either looking to get a jump on advancing bases or possibly stealing second. As he inched down the first-second baseline, he almost baited the left-handed Embree to attempt to pick him off.

Embree bit. Before entering his pitching motion, he threw the ball to Todd Helton, the Rockies' first baseman. Embree had no real expectation of throwing out the Washington base runner. He only intended to keep Kearns closer to first.

Unfortunately, Todd Helton dropped the ball. The Washington Nationals' base runner had little choice. He took off for second.

When Helton recovered the ball, he tossed it to second. Sensing the dilemma, Kearns knew he needed to head back towards first. Fortunately for Colorado, when he did he lost his footing and fell.

While this was happening, Embree raced to insert himself in the situation. He intended to become part of the defensive effort. As luck would have it, he arrived on the scene just where Kearns fell. The second baseman tossed him the ball and Embree quickly tagged the base runner for the final out of the Nationals' eighth inning at bat. Embree never threw a pitch.

In the bottom of the eighth, the Colorado Rockies were able to tally a run. In another strategic move, Rockies' manager Jim Tracy opted for another relief pitcher before the top of the ninth. Thus, Embree was out of the game, and three-outs later the game was over. As Embree was "the pitcher who last pitched prior to the half-inning when the winning team took the lead for the last time," the official scorer deemed him the winner even though he never threw a pitch.

This was not the first time it occurred, but it is rare. Thus, the media drew much attention to this quirk. Even his teammates and fans made light of the situation, as if somehow the baseball Gods had given Embree a gift. At this particular "snapshot" in time, they appeared to have done just that.

While Embree seemed to have received "something for nothing" that is not the case if you consider the entire body of his work. He was somewhat of a journeyman in Major League Baseball. Drafted by the Cleveland Indians in 1992 directly out of Prairie High School (Brush Prairie, Washington), he had two tours of duty in the minors, a stint with the Indians, and then appearances with eight other Major League teams. Eventually, in 2009 he arrived in Colorado to play for the Rockies.

Embree made relief appearances in hundreds of Major League games (878, to be exact). While he tallied a single "pitchless" win, he also managed dozens of legitimate ones (some in come-from-behind fashion). In addition, there were the countless games where his efforts served to stave off a desperate opponents bid for comeback. Moreover, there were all the times the official record merely deemed he "appeared" but gave him no real credit for providing incredible effort to position another for the win.

Yes, in a particular game, Alan Embree notched a pitching win without having thrown a pitch. In viewing just that moment, it might appear like a fluke or a gift. There is no doubt, however, that somewhere along the line he earned that win – though at the time he might have been playing for another team.

Life is similar. In it, you will garner many achievements over time – some great, some small, some already attained and others yet to happen. Of all your achievements, some will come to you very easily, almost like gifts from above. While likely in doubt along the way, some you have had to work incredibly hard to attain (and some will never happen, despite your best effort). Moreover, many, many more will fall somewhere in between those extremes. Whatever the case, whatever the achievement and no matter how you achieved it, commemorate the accomplishment. No doubt, you earned it somehow, some way.

Chapter 10
Life Is A Decathlon

Success Is A Function Of Trying To Do Consistently Well At Everything.

They called him the "Iron Man of Asia." Yang Chuan-kwang or C.K. Yang was born in 1933 to the indigenous Ami Tribe, located in Taiwan, a Republic of China. He became well known as a track star, competing in the decathlon.

The decathlon is a track and field competition involving ten events – five on each of two successive days. Performances in the ten events are scored by reference to a points table. The individual accumulating the highest number of points after the 10 events is declared the winner.

From an early age, Yang demonstrated a proficiency in sports and athletics. His abilities were so outstanding that his coach recognized these talents and quickly introduced him to the decathlon. Yang immediately embraced this challenging multi-day event.

This turned out to be a fortuitous move. Two months later, Yang claimed the gold medal in the 1954 Asian Games. Then four years later he successfully defended his title, winning the 1958 Asian Games. The Republic of China took note of their budding track star. The government granted him support to continue his studies and athletic development at the University of California, Los Angeles (UCLA).

While Yang was considered the greatest athlete of all the Asian nations, he had his sights set higher. The decathlon is a menu of athletic events, testing an individual's speed, endurance, strength, skill and determination. It clearly reflects the ancient Greek ideal of all-around, balanced excellence in sports. The media proclaims the winner of the Olympic Decathlon as the "World's Greatest Athlete."

This title has been bestowed on many Americans, such as Jim Thorpe and two-time Olympic decathlon gold medalist Bob Mathias. No doubt, Yang wanted to add the moniker "World's Greatest" to his list of accomplishments as he prepared to compete in the 1960 Rome Olympics.

On September 5, 1960 in Rome's Estadico Olympico, Yang began his quest to become the Olympic gold medalist in the decathlon. After the first day of competition, he appeared to be well on his way, as he posted the best performance in four of the five events. He had bested his opponents from dozens of nations in the 100-meter dash, long jump, high jump, and 400-meter run.

While day two was not quite as successful, it was close. Heading into the fifth and final event, Yang had posted the best performance in two of the four events, earning top marks in the 110-meter hurdles and pole vault. If he could post a great score in the 1,500-meter run – known as the metric mile and the grueling conclusion to the two-day event – surely he would win the gold medal and be able to proclaim the title "World's Greatest Athlete."

Yang knew this and ran the race of his life. Despite this, however, as darkness settled in on the Italian sky, Yang found himself in second place. He was the silver medalist behind his UCLA teammate, Rafer Johnson.

While Yang had bested Johnson in seven of ten events, success in the decathlon is the measure of consistent excellence. Johnson was competitively close in each of the events that Yang outperformed him. Yang's performance, however, in the other three events – shot put, discus, and javelin – was far and away inferior to that of the eventual gold medalist.

Yang did not win the Olympic gold medal in the decathlon because he was not the best at something. Amongst decathletes, he was the best at lots of things. He did not win the 1960 Olympic decathlon because of significant deficiencies in a few events.

In contrast, Rafer Johnson won the Olympic gold medal not by being the best at any one thing in particular (he only posted the best score in one event – shot put). Rather, he earned the title "World's Greatest Athlete" by posting consistently high marks in all events.

The notion of the decathlon is not limited to the arena of track and field competition, however. Consider almost any other sport or athletic competition. Victory or success generally goes to the well-rounded competitor or team and not the individual or team with a single overpowering attribute.

The notion of the decathlon is not limited to athletic competition. Success in pretty much anything is a function of all-around, balanced excellence and not perfection in any one particular aspect.

Consider parenthood. One is not considered successful by merely being able to provide three nutritious, square meals. And one is not considered successful only by maintaining a safe and healthy home, or simply by devoting the requisite attention to the kids' school work, social anxieties or need to play. No, success in parenting is a function of all of these things. In fact, if one were only competent in one area and deficient in all others, the person would likely be considered a bad parent.

Consider business as well, one is not considered successful by merely having a great product or service. And one is not considered successful only by having an interesting and catchy marketing program, or simply by having a great price, or sound distribution or any other single attribute of business. Success in business requires having the whole package. In fact, each and every year businesses that are great in one aspect and deficient in all others tend to founder or worse.

This notion of the decathlon also holds true for your overall life. There may not necessarily be ten separate attributes to a successful life. A success in life, however, is the measure of multiple attributes.

Being a star at work or in business has little overall meaning unless you are somehow a contributor to the community.

Making a wonderful contribution to the community is nice, but there also needs to be a commitment to faith.

Commitment to community and faith is great, but that effort is somewhat hollow unless you impose a similar effort to be a good neighbor and family member.

Being an outstanding neighbor and member of the family is laudable, but you also need to focus on your own physical and mental well being by taking care of yourself and continuing to learn and develop.

Life is a decathlon. You do not need to be the best at any one thing. You simply need to try to do consistently well at everything.

Chapter 11
An Awesome Kick

You Have Wonderful Talents. Use Them Wherever You Can Add Value.

Anna Powell was never the star player for the Ridgewood High School girls' soccer team. Much of her four years in the program, she spent in the shadows of the school's all-time soccer greats. That, however, did not stop her from developing an awesome kick.

It did not necessarily start in the awesome category, however. Like many, her kick began as simply decent. That is, it was nothing remarkable. Nevertheless, it was good enough for her to contribute to the Generals' girls' soccer team her first three seasons.

As she progressed through the program, she worked on that kick. Powell developed herself physically. She worked on her technique. She took the time to envision herself as having a powerful kick.

In the fall of 2012, when the dust finally settled on her high school soccer career, Powell's work on her kick paid dividends. Her kick helped her score nine goals as a midfielder. It contributed to the Ridgewood High School girls' soccer program having its best season ever – 10-4-2 – her senior year. Her awesome kick was part of the reason the East District of the Ohio Scholastic Soccer Coaches Association awarded her All-District honorable mention honors.

In addition, it earned her a varsity letter on the school's football team. That is correct. Not only did she earn four varsity letters as a soccer player, her senior year the Ridgewood Generals football program also took advantage of Powell's awesome kick.

Midway through the football season, the Ridgewood football program lost its starting kicker to an injury. This seemed to be devastating, as the Generals needed a kicker. After all, the program was hopeful of making the Ohio High School Athletic Association football playoffs for a tenth consecutive season as well as competing for another Inter-Valley Conference title.

Generals' head football coach John Slusser began tryouts amongst several young men on his squad. This exercise, however, appeared more like a comedy routine than a serious competition for a starting position on a regional high school football power. Footballs sailed wide left. Footballs sailed wide right. Some balls barely made it off the ground. Few consistently split the uprights.

Watching the tryout debacle was Ridgewood High School's Athletic Director, Alan Keesee. He could see the frustration on Coach Slusser's face. It was clear. There were no viable kickers amongst the football players. He pondered to himself, "How do you contend for a conference title without a key element of the kicking game?"

As this near tragedy was unfolding, however, the Ridgewood girls' soccer team was making its way toward the field. The Lady Generals had a home match for which it was preparing. Hoping to help the football team, Keesee hailed Casey Claxon, the team's coach, and asked, "Hey coach do you have anybody on your soccer team who could kick extra points?"

As he motioned towards Anna Powell, Coach Claxon casually responded, "Sure, this one right here could."

With no other real options, the special teams coach, Chris Cabot, motioned for Powell to come onto the field for an impromptu tryout. Like a scene out of Hollywood, everything stopped. The entire football team stood quietly in anticipation. The Lady Generals gathered to support their teammate. Even fans heading to the soccer match paused to take in a little bonus entertainment for their admission money.

The pressure seemed to be on Powell. She, however, carried on completely undaunted. She had an awesome kick and she had swung that right foot thousands of times.

With no warm-up, no practice kicks, and never having kick a football before in her life – BOOM! – she nailed her first attempt. As the ball sailed through the uprights, a varsity football player signified his approval of the situation by shouting, "Put a helmet on her!"

Powell's tryout was not over, however. The football coaching staff wanted to see if the first kick was merely a fluke. Assuming she was for real, they were interested to know how much potential Powell's awesome kick had.

They had her take another kick, this time five yards back. She boomed another on target and over the crossbar with plenty of room to spare.

They backed her up again for another attempt. BOOM! The results were the same – field goal. Then again – another field goal further back yet. And again. And again.

Finally, Powell missed. At this point, however, she was almost 40 yards away.

Cheers were erupting from football players, soccer teammates, and on-looking soccer fans. The football coaches were stunned by what they saw. Coach Claxon, however, was not. In a matter-of-fact fashion, he gathered up his senior. He needed her awesome kick for a soccer match the Lady Generals were about to play.

As the soccer match wore on, no doubt, Anna Powell's ears were burning. The football coaches were busy organizing their thoughts and plans for recruiting Ridgewood High's recently discovered placekicking talent. Athletic Director Keesee gave a thumbs-up – there was no rule preventing a girl from playing football.

Shortly after the soccer match was over, special teams Coach Cabot sought out soccer Coach Claxon with one simple question, "Can we ask Anna Powell to kick for the football team?"

With a proud smile, Claxon responded, "Absolutely."

Then Cabot approached Powell. After a quick consultation with her parents, the soccer player with an awesome kick said, "Yes." She agreed to be the first female athlete to play varsity football at Ridgewood High School.

On most nights in the fall, you could find Anna Powell home studying. After all, she was now a two-sport athlete. As she wanted to maintain her 4.0 grade point average, she needed this time to keep up with a full load of classes.

On Thursday evenings, she slipped shin guards into her socks and pulled on a number 11 jersey. She was a Lady General. Powell intended to use her awesome kick to win soccer matches around the West Lafayette, Ohio area for Ridgewood High.

On Friday nights, she was again playing for the benefit of Ridgewood High. On these evenings, however, she wore number 99 and somewhat veiled her feminine identify under a football helmet and a pair of shoulder pads. Nevertheless, she still wielded an awesome kick.

In the fall of 2012, in a small Ohio town where football players reign supreme, Anna Powell was the biggest celebrity of all. As the football seniors headed to the middle school before the final home game in the tradition of signing autographs for the future Generals and their fans, she had the longest line on the team. It seems that size, strength, and speed are nice. They are, however, nothing compared to a girl with an awesome kick.

Your talents may not include an awesome kick. Nevertheless, you have talents. No doubt, the talents you have are wonderful, if not awesome. Whatever the talent, however, and no matter how great (or not) it may be, use your talents.

Do not assume, however, that your talents are only useful for one particular job or activity. Open your mind and share your talents with those around you. In fact, use your talents wherever you can add value. Whatever your talents are, use them wherever they are needed. If you do, you will become the superstar.

Chapter 12
Fourth & 15 Years

You Are Never Too Far Down To Mount A Comeback.

Beloit Daily News Correspondent reporter, Tom Mikolyzk started his Monday, November 8th, 1982 column about the local liberal arts college's football team, "With 8 minutes and 19 seconds to go in the third quarter Saturday afternoon, Beloit College's Buccaneers seemed doomed to another near miss." That was a fair statement, as the team trailed visiting Lake Forest College 31-3. The game appeared out of reach.

Heading into Saturday afternoon's contest against the Lake Forest College, the Buccaneers had posted four wins and four losses. The team was hopeful that it could post its first winning season in 15 years, but it did not appear to be.

This, however, was nothing new. For years, the Beloit College football team was nothing short of hapless. There was losing season after losing season. Moreover, most seasons the Buccaneers could only muster up a couple of wins and many of its losses were drubbings.

The prospects of creating a winner started to change in the summer of 1977. Ed DeGeorge left the defensive coordinator position at his alma mater Colorado College to become the head football coach at Beloit College. He brought with him a handpicked staff and a winning attitude.

After suffering through a winless 1977 season, DeGeorge began a relentless recruiting campaign. It paid off. The Buccaneers finished each of the next two seasons – 1978 and 1979 – with four wins and four losses. While they were not winning seasons, they were not losing seasons either.

In an effort to move beyond being .500, DeGeorge added a ninth game to the 1980 season. Ironically, however, the team finished 4-4-

1. Then in the 1981 campaign, the team finished the season with four wins and five losses, losing the season finale late in the game.

Beloit College still searched for that first winning season and hoped that it would happen in 1982. Those hopes, however, were fading. Behind by 28 points nearly halfway through the third quarter, it seemed almost certain that the Buccaneer football team would suffer its fifth loss. Many of the only few hundred fans who had ventured to Strong Stadium for the game were now heading towards the exits.

At this point, a team's spirit teeters on a precipice. That spirit either falls into an abyss, or that spirit can become inspired. Led by senior captain Bob Larson, the Buccaneers raised their disappointed heads and pulled out of its funk. They were not ready to concede.

This was the final game of the season and for some the final game of a lifetime. They might be going down, but it would not be without a fight. Every member of the team got off the bench, toed the sidelines, and began cheering as if each play were the one that would seal the victory. An inspiration began to spread.

With 4:40 to go in the third quarter, Beloit College senior Tom O'Neill picked off a Lake Forest pass. That fueled the excitement. The team wasted no time capitalizing on it. Junior quarterback Todd Wingrove threw a 44-yard touchdown pass to freshman Mark Meissner. Adding the point-after-touchdown, the Buccaneers now only trailed 31-10.

After an enthused deep kick-off, the Buccaneers defense was determined to hold strong. Three plays later, they gave Lake Forest no real choice but to punt. This further aroused their spirits. Beloit College senior Tony Williamson took advantage of this and burst through the line. He blocked the punt, setting up the offense for a short touchdown run, narrowing the deficit to only 15 points after a failed extra point attempt.

Then the special teams contributed to the cause, forcing a fumble on the ensuing kick-off. After a couple productive passes, an unsportsmanlike call against Lake Forest and a series of runs by senior Brad Huber, the Buccaneers were six points closer. Despite a failed two-point conversion, optimism continued to run high on the Beloit College sidelines, trailing only 31-22.

Taking the field again, the Buccaneer defense continued to do its part. In three plays, it had driven the Lake Forest offense backwards, forcing another punt. This set the Beloit College offense up for another productive drive.

Freshman running back Dave Davis scooted into the end zone standing up and completely untouched. Everything seemed to be working. Even a botched extra-point kick resulted in a two-point conversion for the Buccaneers. They were now only behind by a single point: 31-30.

With only 3:54 remaining in the game, the Buccaneer defense made one more unyielding stand, forcing Lake Forest to punt. Then the Beloit College offense set about executing another well-orchestrated drive. It maneuvered the ball down field and appeared to be positioning itself for a field goal – running the ball for short gains in the middle of the field as the time ticked away.

A field goal was not in the game plan, however. With 21 seconds, quarterback Todd Wingrove faked a handoff. As the Lake Forest defense converged on the ruse, Wingrove calmly darted a pass to his receiver who was wide open in the end zone.

On November 6th, 1982, the Beloit College Buccaneers never gave up. In so doing, they had completed a 28-point comeback. This comeback did not just win the game, but it ensured the first winning football season in 15 years for the college.

The lesson in this game is that you are never too far down to mount a comeback. No matter what the situation is, never give up. Life may throw disappointments at you. Do not let that deter you. March on.

From time to time, you will find yourself behind – sometimes by a little and sometimes by a lot. Whatever the case, it is never too much. Lead with your chin and keep moving forward. This does not guarantee that your comeback will be successful, but it always gives you a chance.

Even if ultimately the comeback fails, however, you will still have achieved something. You will no doubt generate a sense of pride for yourself and, likely, the respect of others. You might even build momentum that will carry over as you're going into that next "thing," be it a game, a proposal, or opportunity.

While much of this sounds like "coach" speak, there is much truth in it. Life is comprised of hundreds of contests and encounters. In fact, you can view life as dozens of segments or seasons. From time to time, you will find yourself behind. Whatever the case, you are never too far down to mount a comeback. As long as you continue to make an effort, you are not out of it.

With that determined effort, there is always a chance. There is always a chance that you can claim victory. However you might define it, there is always a chance you can achieve a winning season.

Chapter 13
McNasty

Your Talent Is Important, But Not More Important Than Your Character.

John McEnroe was an icon. Seemingly, out of nowhere, he burst onto the tennis scene. After graduating from Manhattan's Trinity School in 1977, he qualified for Wimbledon. More than qualifying, however, he became the youngest player to reach the semifinals, losing to Jimmy Connors.

Later that summer, he enrolled at Stanford University on a scholarship. That year, he led the Cardinal tennis team to a national championship, winning the singles championship in the process.

Conquering everything he could on the college tennis scene, McEnroe turned pro. Within a year, he was achieving notable success. In 1979, he captured his first U.S. Open, winning the final in straight sets.

The following year, he battled four-time champion Bjorn Borg in the 1980 Wimbledon final. Down two sets to one, and trailing 5-4 in the fourth set, McEnroe refused to lose. Continuing to compete, he evened up the score 6-6.

This led to a classic championship match. As the tiebreaker continued, McEnroe saved five championship points before eventually prevailing, 18-16. Although McEnroe lost the fifth set 8-6, he established himself as a formidable tennis professional.

On July 4, 1981, he again found himself in Wimbledon against Borg – now the five-time champion. McEnroe attacked. He beat the reigning Wimbledon champion in just four sets, which also ended Borg's 41-match winning streak.

This victory was no fluke. A year later McEnroe again beat Borg in the U.S. Open. In so doing, he made a case for himself as one of the world's elite tennis players. His success continued.

He was the key to the U.S. winning the Davis Cup in 1981 And he was the first since Don Budge in 1938 to sweep the singles at Wimbledon, the U.S. Open and the Davis Cup final. In 1984, McEnroe blew away the competition, compiling an astounding 82-3 record and winning 13 tournaments (a career-high that included his third Wimbledon and fourth U.S. Open).

When his tennis career was complete, he had made $12,539,622 in official earnings. In so doing, he claimed 77 singles titles, which was the third most in professional tennis history – behind Jimmy Connors (109) and Ivan Lendl (94). Additionally, he won 17 Grand Slam championships (including nine in men's doubles and mixed doubles at the French Open). Finally, he helped the U.S. win five Davis Cups, compiling a remarkable record of 41-8 in singles and 18-2 in doubles.

John McEnroe was an icon. Unfortunately, however, his iconic status was less about his athletic prowess and more about his conduct. Seemingly, match after match, tournament after tournament, McEnroe overshadowed his tennis achievements with outrageous outbursts against and foul language towards tennis officials and referees.

While he could have established himself as a hardworking, tenacious competitor (something fans of any sport appreciate and tennis fans adore), he tarnished his personal brand with antics. While this led to countless fines and occasional disqualifications, the consequences were likely more damaging than McEnroe could imagine.

For starters, the media furthered his infamy. Reporters and writers shared their sentiments, calling him "Superbrat," "McNasty," and "Crybaby."

He came across as a precocious brat -- immensely talented, spoiled and rather obnoxious. On the court, he pouted, cursed, threw his racket. . . . He was a crybaby. Off court, he demonstrated little *savoir faire*. Barry Lorge, *The Washington Post*

McEnroe does most of his pouting on the courts. In private, this devastating athlete can be a nice enough kid . . . but when he steps to the service line, with his perpetually put-upon expression and his insistence that every line call and crowd reaction go his way, his public posture is all too easy to understand. Call it spoiled. Pete Axthelm *Newsweek*

The real damage, however, was financial. During his tennis career, professional athletes worldwide were making millions from lucrative advertising campaigns, product endorsements, and sponsorship deals. McEnroe, however, saw very little. As one president of a Madison Avenue ad agency put it, "When I see McEnroe, I see 'bad sport.' I wouldn't want him identified with my product."

No doubt, John McEnroe was a tennis talent. From that, he won hundreds of matches and dozens of tournaments around the world. While his talent won in tennis, his character cost him. It cost him in terms of respect amongst his peers. It cost him in terms of fans that could never identify with his behavior. It cost him in terms of off-court earnings from his name and potential image.

Know this: Your talent – with whatever it is you do – is important. It, however, is nowhere near as important as the character with which you display that talent.

To be great, you need to bolster your talents with kindness for those around you. You also need to compliment your talent with a degree of reverence. In addition, you need to combine your talent with integrity, fairness and a whole bunch of other things. In short, to be truly great, you need to be a good person.

Chapter 14
Still The Best Policy

Nothing Can Beat The Honest Person.

In the fall of 2005, Adam Van Houten was a sophomore at Mount Gilead High School in Mount Gilead – a small town in north central Ohio. On October 14th and 15th, he was competing in the Ohio high school state golf championship, being held at the Firefox Golf Club, just south of Columbus.

After two days of play, Adam was in the clubhouse with a seven-stroke lead over all of the other golfers who had finished. The Division II state championship was all but a certainty for him. In fact, there was only one person on the course who had a realistic chance of even tying Adam – forcing a play-off.

However, as Adam was waiting, something happened. On the official score board was his name followed by the number 74 – his score for the second round of the state championship.

As he was mulling over his final round of golf, something did not seem right in his mind. Although he would have normally kept for his own record an unofficial tally of his score, the one he was keeping for this round of play was taken somewhere by a gust of wind on the first nine holes. However, even without this he felt that something was wrong with the posted score.

After quickly consulting with his coach and father on his own, he went to the Ohio High School Athletic Association officials and asked to check his scorecard. According to Ohio high school golf championship protocol, each player records the scores of his playing partner.

After the round is complete, each player then checks the tally the other player kept. Assuming it is correct, the player signs the card to indicate that it is accurate and authentic. Under OHSAA rules, however, in golf each player is "responsible for the correctness of the score for each hole on his score card."

It did not take Adam long to discover what was troubling him. Although he had checked his card twice before signing it, on the 10th hole of his final round, his playing partner had entered a five for his score. He, along with help from his father, who followed his son shot by shot for the entire round, reviewed in his mind the details of the 10th hole. Although distraught, Adam clearly determined that his score for this hole should have been a six, instead of a five.

Adam quickly disclosed the error to the OHSAA officials. Thus, his final round should have been a 75 and not a 74, making his total 36-hole tournament score a 145 rather than a 144. As the next closest competitor posted a 151, Adam's score would have still been enough for the OHSAA to declare Adam the Division II champion.

However, because he had already signed his scorecard, OHSAA officials had no choice but to disqualify Adam, even though they were tickled by his honesty. Rather than being crowned state champion, Adam's name had a prominent "DQ" next to it on the scoreboard.

If Adam had kept quiet, no one would have ever known about the scorecard error. No one would have even suspected anything. Adam would have been the 2005 OHSAA Division II Boy's Golf Champion.

While Adam might carry some guilt with him for not admitting the error that disqualified him, if we put that aside we know with a degree of certainty what types of awards and accolades a high school golf champion garners. The OHSAA would have given Adam a medal to hang around his neck and he would have gone down in the record book as state champion.

Further, everyone at the event would have congratulated him and held him in high esteem. We need to remember, however, that he would have had to share that spotlight with the champions from other divisions as well as the team champions.

Adam would have certainly been welcomed back at Mount Gilead High School as a conquering hero, as state championships do not happen often in most communities. This fanfare would not have lasted long, however, as the end of the Ohio high school golf championships coincides with the start of high school football playoffs and the start of basketball, wrestling and other sports.

The community of Mount Gilead itself might erect a small sign on each major road leading into the limits announcing "Home Of Adam Van Houten, 2005 Ohio High School Division II State Golf Champion." This, however, would soon become just another sign that people drive by and ignore as irrelevant.

Certainly, there would be an article in the paper about Adam's achievement. The article, however, would have only been in the local paper, *Morrow County Sentinel*. Moreover, the article would likely only be a few short paragraphs, as it would be competing with important local activities and other sporting events.

Nevertheless, Adam did not win the Ohio High School Division II State Golf Championship. His character, honesty, and courage would not allow it. Adam, and Adam alone, saw that the OSHAA had posted a 74 when he knew, somehow, that the score should have been 75. He alone took action to review his scorecard. He alone disclosed his error to OHSAA officials when he discovered it. What did this honesty gain him?

No, Adam did not get a medal from the OHSAA. However, the Mount Gilead Exempt Local School Board of Education officially recognized Adam for his achievement and sportsmanship and gave him a plaque declaring him "Our State Champion."

Although Adam did not stay at the OHSAA Golf Championships long enough to realize it, his honesty created an atmosphere of admiration. As he embarked upon his junior and senior year of high school golf, many of those whom he competed against (as well as their coaches and fans) greeted him with congratulations and held Adam in high esteem. Moreover, he will not have to share the spotlight with anyone else.

Despite the disqualification, Adam was welcomed back at Mount Gilead High School as more than just a conquering hero. His friends and classmates were able to look beyond the technical disqualification and recognize that he was truly the best high school Division II golfer in Ohio. Beyond that, however, they acknowledged Adam for what he truly is: honest and courageous. This is something that they will always see in Adam no matter what sport is teeing up or kicking off.

While there may be no plans for a sign announcing Adam's championship achievement at the Mount Gilead Village limits, members of the community recognized him in other ways. A car dealership purchased a large space in the local paper. In the space was a picture of Adam along with the words "In Ohio – Integrity Has A New Spelling. It is spelled: Adam Van Houten."

Deb Clauss, Mount Gilead High School principal, will tell anyone who asks, "Yes, this young man is one of my students. The story is correct – and we are very proud of the actions of this young man. ... He is a great example of integrity and ethics in sports!"

As you might guess, there was an article in the paper about Adam's honesty. There was a rather lengthy article in the *Morrow County Sentinel*. There was also another one in the *Mansfield News Journal*. Moreover, there was another one in the *Columbus Dispatch* by sports columnist Bob Hunter. Normally, devoting time to remarking about the Ohio State Buckeyes, Columbus Blue Jackets or professionals sports teams from Cleveland and Cincinnati, Hunter wrote of Adam:

How do you measure a champion? By scores or by sportsmanship? By hardware or by honor? By medals or by principle? Adam Van Houten is not a state golf champion. He doesn't have the hardware or the medals, doesn't have the title or the line in the record book. But Van Houten ... has integrity, and that's at least as important.

Clearly, the awards and accolades of honesty have proved far more beneficial to Adam than those of a state high school golf championship. However, this same lesson holds true for everyone.

On October 15, 2005, Adam Van Houten started the second round of the Ohio State High School Golf Championships. On that day, his intention was simple – to win the OHSAA Division II state golf championship. If you check the record book, officially it did not happen.

On that day, Adam did not intend to become an icon for honesty, values, and courage in high school athletics and in a small Ohio community. Fate, however, intervened and he did.

On that day, what Adam did do, whether he realizes it or not, was perform an important experiment. Somewhere on the 10th hole of Foxfire Golf Course during the 2005 OHSAA Division II Golf Championship, someone made what amounted to nothing more than a clerical error. A couple hours later, Adam complicated that mistake with his own minor oversight. These two elements, however, set the stage to test the cliché "honesty is the best policy."

Honesty is the best policy – in sports, in life, and in business. Whether you are seeking employment, gainfully employed or looking to grow a business, sooner or later you will be faced with a moral dilemma of one sort or another. When you do, you always need to do the right thing. As Adam Van Houten's story illustrates, in the long-run it will be the most profitable and respected course of action.

Chapter 15
Do You Believe In Miracles?

Success In Life Is Driven By Things Other Than Miracles.

During the height of the cold war, the Soviet Union built a hockey dynasty. Beginning in the early 60's, the Soviet national hockey team was virtually unbeatable at the amateur level. They had won every Olympic gold medal since the 1964 games, overpowering every opponent in the process. The Soviet hockey machine even held its own against professionals, basically tying the NHL All-Stars in a multi-game series.

With the 1980 Lake Placid Olympic Games fast approaching, the Soviet hockey team was again the favorite for gold. In fact, they expected to manhandle the competition, as much of their veteran 1976 Gold Medal team was back.

While potential rivals were mentioned – teams like Sweden, Czechoslovakia and West Germany – this was merely done in an attempt to create a meager amount of intrigue for the event. In short, there was no one that had a chance against the Soviet hockey juggernaut, least of all the United States.

In fact, the young American team – comprised of mere college players and NHL long shots – was given no chance against the Soviet squad. Further bolstering this conclusion was the fact that the Soviet Union had pounded the Americans 10-3 in an exhibition game at Madison Square Garden the week before the start of the Olympic games.

Despite the long odds, the Americans faced off against the Soviets in the opening game of the medal round.

Despite being outmatched, the Americans met every challenge posed by the Soviets.

Despite being out shot, the Americans found themselves tied with the Soviets half way through the third and final period.

On February 22, 1980, the long shot, out matched, out shot American team scored with 10 minutes to play to take a 4-3 lead against the Soviet Union. A lead they hung on to for the remainder of the game. As the final seconds ticked away, announcer Al Michaels exclaimed (as this country held its collective breath), "DO YOU BELIEVE IN MIRACLES? YES!

This remains as one of the most famous calls in sports broadcasting history. This performance touched the hearts of Americans like no other. This victory served to galvanize the pride and patriotism of this country at a time when we needed it most.

This will be forever known as "The Miracle On Ice."

This, however, was no miracle. There are no miracles in sports – God reserves miracles for parting of Red Seas and feeding thousands with a few fish.

The Miracle On Ice was no miracle. Rather, it was destiny.

The Americans may have lacked experience, but they did not lack a vision. Coach Herb Brooks clearly reinforced that from the moment he assembled the team.

The Soviet hockey army may have outmatched the Americans, but that never stopped the American players from believing. They knew that collectively they possessed a unique talent that would ensure their success.

Everyone may have discounted the Americans, but that did not dampen their commitment to put forth the necessary hard work.

The Miracle On Ice was simply destiny and not really some miraculous event. So what is the point?

Simple. Every day life is much like sports. Wondrous success in business, career, or personal life can, does, and hopefully will happen. Nothing miraculous, however, is going to drive your business, career, or personal life to the success you want.

As the 1980 United States Olympic Hockey gold medal demonstrates, it is simply that phenomenal things can and will occur whenever you have the:

Courage to have a consistent vision of the success you want; and,

Confidence to have an unwavering belief that your abilities are special and uniquely designed to help you succeed; and,

Discipline to maintain an untiring work ethic to propel you towards your goals.

In summary, if you find and maintain this level of *courage, confidence*, and *discipline*, there is no doubt that one day you will experience a "DO YOU BELIEVE IN MIRACLES?" kind of day. When it happens, however, remember that it was no miracle. Rather you created that destiny.

Chapter 16
Unstoppable

The Only Limitations You Really Have, Are The Ones You Impose On Yourself.

The British military deployed Phil Packer to Iraq in order to establish some stability to the region. While the 36-year-old made it out alive, he was one of the estimated tens of thousands who suffered a battle-related injury.

In February 2008, Packer's base near Basra, Iraq came under rocket fire. The attack sent a vehicle rolling down a sand bank. It struck the 16-year military veteran and dragged him under it.

Heroic medical attention saved his life. He, however, had to endure recovery in a hospital for more than four months. The ordeal left Packer with no feeling or motor control in his legs, and no bladder or bowel control.

Doctors told him that he would never walk again. He did not listen. At little over a year later, he competed in the 2009 London Marathon, finishing the grueling 26.2-mile race on crutches in about 13 days (this was after rowing the English Channel).

In 1990, Dustin Carter's parents brought him into this world just like any other happy, healthy little boy. Unfortunately, by age five, he contracted a rare blood disease. In time, this would claim both his legs and much of his arms.

The blood disease, however, did nothing to his heart. He refused to accept any limitations that this medical misfortune might have otherwise brought. He insisted on being a normal kid.

Carter attended a normal school. He refused to ride anything other than the bus all the other kids rode. And he insisted on wrestling.

As a student at Hillsboro High School (60 miles east of Cincinnati, Ohio), Carter was on the varsity wrestling team. Initially the sports and his fully functioning competition seemed to provide an insurmountable challenge for him. He persevered. In working hard at becoming more mobile and converted his limitations into assets.

By his senior season, Carter was seemingly unstoppable. At the 103-weight class, he won match after match after match. In so doing, he earned title after title after title. Conference champion. District champion. Regional champion.

In February 2008, Carter did something that few believe anyone with his limitations could. He earned a place to compete in the Ohio High School Athletic Association meet. While he ultimately lost in the quarterfinals, in February 2008 he completed his final year of wrestling with an incredible 41-2 record.

If you stop and think about it, there are averages in life but no true normal. We all come in different shapes, sizes, with all sorts of abilities. Certainly, some are more able-bodied at certain things than others. That said, however, you have no real restrictions in life. The only limitations you have are the ones you impose upon yourself. With whatever you want to do, believe that you can and work to make it happen. You too are unstoppable.

Chapter 17
In The Face Of Tradition

Follow Your Heart And Passionately Do What You Want To Do.

Jessica Stubitsch is just another co-ed at Northern Illinois University, working towards a degree in early childhood education, hoping one day to be a kindergarten teacher. She studies hard, but not as hard as she could if you ask her. She had lots of college life fun, but too much if you ask her mother. Jess is just another co-ed at Northern Illinois University.

When she is not studying or having fun, she is at practice or playing in a game. She is a goalie for the NIU Huskies. That, however, is not so unusual either. Since the passage of Title IX in 1972 (granting both sexes equal educational opportunities in publically funded entities), young women have been participating in sports in growing numbers in high schools and universities across the country.

Besides participating in sports is part of who Jess is. She began participating at a young age. In high school, she earned a varsity letter playing soccer for Johnsburg High School, north of Chicago. In addition to being a soccer player for the lady Skyhawks, she was active in quite a few intramural sports throughout high school, including floor hockey and softball. As her high school did not have a hockey program, Jess played on a consolidated women's high school team as well as within Team Illinois women's hockey program.

What sets Jess apart, however, is that she plays goalie on the men's hockey team at NIU. She looked at many schools, but in the end did not want to give up hockey. She had an opportunity to play hockey for a women's team at Northern Michigan University, but opted to sign on with the NIU Huskies. While there was no guarantee, she challenged herself to make the men's team, knowing it would make her a better goalie in the end.

She is no token member of the team. She practices and works in the off-season with the team. Jess travels with the team, sees game action, and dutifully takes her time "riding the pines." The coaches even rely on her to help in the recruiting process, because she is such a great example of someone who can enjoy campus life, play a collegiate sport, and still make the grade. All in all, however, she is just another co-ed at NIU.

Morgan Van Lanen is also typical – a typical American teen. She has lots of friends and they talk, text and chat like most any other teenage girl. She dresses up and goes to school dances. And she likes being with her family. Morgan is a dancer.

No, that is not completely accurate. She was a dancer. Her mother enrolled her in dance and wanted her to continue with it. In fact, her mother begged her to stay involved. Morgan, however, begged harder to escape the world of tutus and tap shoes.

Her mother tried to bribe her to stay in dance, with offers of ribbons, bows, and beautiful outfits. She was unmoved. Ultimately, Morgan's grandfather – bribing her to excel at her athletic passion –helped her cut ties with the world of dance forever.

When Morgan was in second grade, she was walking down the hall at school with her parents. As they walked past the gymnasium, they noticed that a family friend was coaching youth wrestlers in the area. Innocently, they stopped in to say hello.

After a few moments of chit chat, the coach suggested that Morgan join. Of course, Morgan's parents laughed in unison almost as if to say, "Wrestling is for boys." The coach did not laugh. He defended, "Wrestling is not just for boys. Morgan should give it a try."

That is exactly what Morgan did. She attended a couple practices and found that she liked it. It was as if wrestling ignited a fire inside her to compete. Thus, the more she wrestled, the more she enjoyed it.

The more she enjoyed it, the more she improved. Of course, the more she improved, the more she won. As there were few girl wrestlers, the more she left a wake of distraught boys who had to deal with the fact that they had been beaten by a girl.

Moreover, Morgan's grandfather added some incentive to an already enthusiastic grappler. In her sixth grade year, he offered her a dollar for every time she pinned an opponent. Inspired, Morgan led the team in that statistic, recording a school record 26 pins and only 2 or 3 losses. The world of ballet, tap and hip hop did not stand a chance.

Morgan is not a dancer. She is a Bronco. A full-fledged member of the Bark River-Harris High School wrestling team. Dan Seronko, Morgan's high school coach raves, "This young gal has a big heart and a die-hard attitude. She works very hard and never quits. She has set goals for herself and is well on her way there."

As Erin DiMeglio walks into the High School gym fans of the girls volleyball team greet her with high-fives and chants of her name. Unfortunately she can't stay. She has to get to football practice. She is not a manager or student trainer hoping to be near the game or the men who play it. Erin is a third-string quarterback for the South Plantation Paladins.

The football program is not a hapless one that takes any warm body. South (known as this to avoid confusion with Plantation High School) is a large high school near Fort Lauderdale, Florida. It has plenty of young men who want to be part of its football program.

South does not compete in some inept conference where teams build their rosters by recruiting athletes from other sports and activities. Most of the high schools are in Florida's Class 8A, which is roughly equivalent to the lower end NCAA Division III. Most teams produce each year a plethora of major college football talent.

Erin is not on the team to make a statement that "girls have the right to do anything that boys can do." Rather Coach Doug Gatewood, needing a third-string quarterback, recruited her off the high school's flag football program for girls. She developed her skills and toughness from participating in high school basketball, through sibling rivalry, and by living in a neighborhood of athletes on the lookout to start a pick-up game.

Erin is not just a token third-string, destined to sit the bench. She is part of the game plan. Her coach has insisted that she know the playbook, as she is literally only two plays away from having to command a complicated high school football offense.

In fact, on September 1, 2012, she made Florida high school history. In the season opener, she got in the game and became the State's first female quarterback to play in a regular-season game.

Jessica's incredible saves, Morgan's two-point takedowns, and Erin's darting passes reveals "women are every bit equal to men." Each of these young ladies were not out to prove a point or make a statement. They did not do it to draw attention to themselves. They chose to do something simply because they had a passion to do it.

Their lesson transcends gender, however. Life tends to have accumulated layers of conformity. Such as ...

Established Stereotypes: All politicians think only of personal gain ... Those who are blonde or muscle bound are dense ... Those who like to read or work with computers are geeks; and,

Cultural Traditions: The mother puts her career on hold to stay at home to raise the children ... Monday through Friday is the appropriate work week ... Turkey is served on Thanksgiving; and,

Unfounded Beliefs: You need to have a college degree to be successful ... You need to take vacation ... Watching too much television is bad for you.

No doubt, there might be people and situations you chose to typecast. Additionally, there may be certain standards that are acceptable for you. Moreover, there might be well-established beliefs to which you chose to adhere. There is nothing wrong with any of this.

If, however, for whatever reason you do not agree with any of what some might consider conventional wisdom, do not let that thinking limit you. As long as your actions do not violate a law or willfully hurt another, follow your heart and passionately do what you want to do.

Chapter 18
Four Eighteen

Set Worthwhile Goals, But Keep Going Once You Achieve Them.

The game of football has been around for over 100 years. In that time, there is a plethora of accumulated statistics. From those statistics, those in the game can establish benchmarks that serve to separate mediocrity from greatness. Players, coaches, and even fans know position-by-position what we can consider a notable performance and what is just so-so.

For receivers, a notable performance is 100 yards. If a wide out or tight end catches enough balls and generates enough yards after the catch to accumulate an excess of 100 yards, the football world and media deem that a relatively notable performance. This benchmark is the standard at every level of football, from the professional ranks, through every division of college, and on into high school.

With a hometown in tiny Delaware, Ohio and attending a small private boarding school near St. Louis, major college football programs did not give much attention to Lewis Howes. As such, in the fall of 2001, he opted for an opportunity to play college football in Division III (over mild interest from larger NCAA schools). Nevertheless, he was well aware of the 100-yard standard.

As a consistent player for Principia College, Lewis Howes did not necessarily have the 100-yard benchmark written as an official goal each game. Nevertheless, this milestone was in his mind. Moreover, he approached each contest for the Panthers with the hope and aspiration of achieving it. This was certainly the case on October 12, 2002, when Howes suited up for a game against visiting Martin Luther College Knights.

Following a typically subdued Division III pregame, the Knights kicker knocked the ball into the end zone at Clark Field. Not content to take a touchback, the Panthers return man bolted out of the end zone, making it to the 27 yard line before Martin Luther defenders could stop him.

Howes and his offensive teammates wasted no time. After an incomplete pass and a 12-yard run, Principia's quarterback, hit Howes for an 11-yard completion. The Panthers had the ball at mid-field.

After a one-yard run on first down, Howes caught another pass – 12 more yards. With another set of downs, Martin Luther sacked the Principia quarterback for a ten-yard loss. The quarterback, however, immediately atoned, tossing a 25-yard pass to another Panther receiver and then a 22-yard touchdown to Howes. Although, the Knights blocked the point-after attempt, Principia College led 6-0 and Howes had 55 receiving yards on only three receptions.

Martin Luther attempted to answer, but were unable. They, however, managed to punt the ball out of the end zone, forcing Principia to start on its own 20.

This was merely an inconvenience for Principia. The Panther quarterback completed another pass to Howes, who then stormed over defenders. In a mere 11 seconds, he scored an 80-yard touchdown. With 7:23 left in the 1st quarter, the Panthers led 13-0 and Howes had 135 yards to his credit, well over what he had aspired to at the beginning of the game.

He was not done, however. He couldn't be. Martin Luther was not going to quit. Battling back, they scored a touchdown of their own with a little over a minute in the 1st quarter.

Principia lost over half its lead and Howes knew he needed to raise his personal ambitions for the game. Before the end of the 1st quarter, he caught another pass for 35 yards. This set Howes up to pull in a 34-yard touchdown reception on the first play of the 2nd quarter.

After the extra point, Principia led the Knights 20-7, in large part to Howes' 200-plus receiving yards. He was not done, however. While Principia hoped to avenge the 38-20 loss it suffered a year earlier, Martin Luther did not intend to make it easy.

The Knights double-teamed Principia's star receiver. This defensive effort stymied Howes and the Panther's offense. The Knights, however, were able to generate its own offense. By half time, it led the game 21-20. Then after the opening drive of the 3rd quarter, it extended the lead to 28-20.

Howes and the Panthers tried to respond. He made a few more receptions. Principia was re-gaining some momentum.

Then the Panthers turned the ball over on a fumble. Before it could get it back, they were in a 35-20 hole. Despite Howes' efforts, it appeared as if the game was headed towards a similar result to the 2001 contest.

Neither Howes nor his teammates were accepting of that notion. At this point, Howes had completely lost track of his receiving yardage. Whatever it was, however, it was not enough. The Panthers pushed its offense and Howes worked to break free of double coverage. He generated still more yards and Principia drove the field, narrowing its deficit 35-28 with a minute remaining in the 3rd quarter.

The Panther defense then did its part. Bending, but not breaking, it got the ball back to its offense without surrendering any more points to Martin Luther College.

The Principia offense was determined to even the score and then either win the game outright or do it in overtime. To this point, Howes had made an incredible contribution to the cause – a game to remember. He was not satisfied, however.

He aspired to achieve more as the Panthers drove the football against the Knights. He pulled in a reception for 35 yards. Then another. Then another. Then he pulled in one for a 46-yard touchdown. Following the point-after attempt, Principia had tied the score at 35.

While on the sideline, Howes could only watch as the Martin-Luther offense systematically moved down the field. In 13 plays, they covered 80 yards. The Knights retook the lead – 42-35.

However many yards Howes had accumulated, he knew he would need to generate more. Moreover, the Principia offense had to move fast, as the Knights' last drive whittled over six minutes off the game.

Martin Luther College knew that Howes was the preferred receiver at this point. The Knights assigned a third defender to shadow him.

It did not matter. Pass after pass came in Howes' direction. Most he caught. A few fell incomplete. One was intercepted.

The game appeared lost. The Panther defense, however, forced a fumble. Its offense could resume the drive and they immediately went back towards Howes. Completion. Completion. Completion.

Unfortunately, before Principia could tie the score, it had run out of downs and time. Despite his incredible showing, Howes was devastated. The personal achievement was nice. A win would have made it better.

Nevertheless, when the teams finalized their official tally, Lewis Howes had generated 418 total receiving yards. His having a goal and then continuing to press long after that goal was eclipsed, had allowed him to set an NCAA record for receiving yards for all divisions (breaking the record of 405 yards established by Troy Edwards in 1998 at Louisiana Tech).

To be successful, establish worthwhile goals, whether personal or professional. Keep these goals top-of-mind every day and work hard to achieve them. To be great, however, once you achieve your goals do not stop. Rather press on. Quickly set new goals and get after working hard to achieve those. This will bring you closer to greatness.

Chapter 19
The Wizard Of Westwood

Work Hard. Success Can Be Yours. Just Not Tomorrow.

Ask most anyone to name some coaching legends and the name John Wooden is likely to come up in the conversation. Coach Wooden is best known for being the head basketball coach at the University of California, Los Angeles (UCLA).

In 27 seasons of coaching at UCLA, the Bruins won an astonishing 80% of their games, posting 620 wins against only 147 losses. Through Wooden's leadership, his teams won 10 national titles and countless conference titles.

His teams posted an undefeated record in four different complete seasons – 1963-64, 1966-67, 1971-72, and 1972-73. In fact, from the start of the 1971 season until January 19, 1974, Wooden's Bruins established a still-standing record 88-game winning streak.

In 2003, UCLA renamed its basketball court as The Nell and John Wooden Court at Pauley Pavilion. He was a college basketball icon for years. He will likely be a coaching legend forever. This is how the sporting world remembers John Wooden.

This picture of this coaching marvel is accurate. What the official record of John Wooden often fails to mention, however, is the journey. Wooden established his place in history through hard work and dedication even though his ultimate stature was never guaranteed.

Not surprisingly, Wooden was a great basketball player. In high school, he was a three-year All-State basketball player. In so doing, he helped his team consistently make deep runs into the post-season tournament, including capturing the state championship one year.

After high school, he made his mark as an All-American and team captain playing basketball for Purdue University. Nicknamed the

Indiana Rubber Man, for his hustle and effort, Wooden helped the Boilermakers win two Big Ten Championships and the 1932 NCAA National Championship.

After his career at Purdue, Wooden played professionally for seven years. In those days, however, the pay for professional basketball players was minimal and often unreliable. As such, to make ends meet players needed to find work in the real world as well. For Wooden, he taught high school and helped coach the basketball teams.

When his professional career was over, he began teaching and coaching fulltime. In his first season coaching at Dayton (Kentucky) High School, he had a losing season – posting a 6-11 mark. A year later, he took a new position at Central High School in South Bend, Indiana, racking up a 218-42 record during his tenure there.

Wooden took a hiatus from coaching to join the Navy after the Japanese bombed Pearl Harbor. After four years of service, however, he was back at coaching. He took a position at Indiana State University (then known as Indiana State Teachers' College) where in two seasons he lead the Sycamores to an overall record of 47-14, back-to-back conference titles, and invitations to the National Association of Intercollegiate Athletics (NAIA) tournament.

From here, UCLA offered him the job as head basketball coach. While his Bruin teams captured four consecutive Pacific Coast Conference titles, the next 11 years his teams struggled. There was an occasional tournament title, but there were also years where UCLA barely eked out more wins than losses.

Finally, in 1964 – his 15th year at UCLA – John Wooden's Bruins captured their first NCAA national championship. This championship set in motion his historic run as an elite college basketball coach. While most everyone connected with sports is aware of his stature as a legendary coaching figure, few are aware that he built it bit by bit over an almost 50-year period and ultimately into the Wizard of Westwood.

Success in life is not necessarily easy. It is, however, somewhat formulaic. It requires you to have a large measure of hard work along with a equally sizable dose of commitment and discipline to your chosen trade, profession or vocation. While hard work and discipline are important, you also need to include a hefty degree of patience. Your effort and commitment will garner you the lofty success you want, it just will not happen overnight ... or in a year ... or even a decade, maybe.

Chapter 20
Shoeless Ron Hunter

You Have Influence. However Big Or Small, Use It For Good.

Ron Hunter coaches basketball in his bare feet. He does not do so because he cannot afford shoes. While he is not a high profile coach with a seven-figure annual coaching contract, he leads a relatively comfortable life as the head basketball coach for IUPUI – Indiana University-Purdue University of Indianapolis. In other words, Ron Hunter can afford shoes.

Coach Hunter, rather, commands his Jaguars courtside with no shoes simply because, for many around the world, shoes are a luxury that they go without. Thus, his intent is to generate support for Samaritan's Feet, a Charlotte, North Carolina, Christian-based charity whose mission is to collect and distribute shoes to impoverished kids around the world.

Initially, Hunter felt he set a lofty goal to collect 30,000 pairs of shoes before the end of a January 2008 game against Oakland University. Through working hard, working his connections, and using the support of administrators at IUPUI, by tip-off the shoe tally was at 110,000 pairs and counting.

Students contributed. The United States Department of Homeland Security contributed. Other charities, Wal-Mart, and Nine West contributed. Converse contributed 15,000 pairs during Hunter's appearance on ESPN's popular radio program, Mike & Mike In The Morning.

After the final count, Hunter's antics and influence garnered 140,000 pairs of shoes and $30,000. As impressive as that seems, the coach was not satisfied. In delivering the shoes to Africa, Hunter realized that his efforts – as impressive as they seemed – did not meet the need, as men, women and children were turned away still shoeless.

In 2009, he reached out to his college coaching brethren. While Hunter may have been the only one coaching barefoot, others joined in to collect shoes for those in need and to bring attention to Samaritan's Feet. The goal of their cumulative influence: Collect over one million pairs of shoes.

While you might not be a college basketball coach, you have influence. While you might not have access to national radio programs, you have influence. Whoever you are and whatever you do, you have influence over others. Whether that influence is big or small, use it to do something positive in the world.

Chapter 21
Stand Tall!

You Are Great In Your Own Right.
Bow Before No Earthly King.

The crowning spectacle of any Olympic Games is the opening ceremonies. No matter what Olympic sport you happen to be a fan (or even if you are a fan of no sport at all), this exhibition is captivating, entertaining and inspiring.

Traditionally, with words encouraging world peace and good sportsmanship, the head of state of the host nation officially announces the start of the opening ceremony. From there, nation after nation enter the stadium, each being led by an athlete representative that carries that country's flag. As each country proceeds around the infield, when they pass where the head of state is seated, following tradition, the flag bearer dips the nation's flag in deference to the host country's lead dignitary.

Every nation follows this protocol – every nation but the United States. This exception to the tradition is considered tradition in and of itself and it relates back over 100 years to the 1908 London Games.

On July 14 at approximately 2:45 PM, with Austria leading the way, nations began to parade into London's White City Stadium for the opening ceremonies of the 1908 Olympic Games. Eventually, the United States joined the procession, being led by 6'6", 275 pound Ralph Rose as its flag bearer.

As the contingent of Americans marched before King Edward VII, to the outrage of the crowd, Rose refused to lower the American flag as was custom. Although there is some debate as to just how much of an uproar this created amongst the British, one American's response to the act was clear. Martin Sheridan, known as a burly, hot-tempered shot putter, emphatically stated, *"This flag dips to no earthly king."*

As such, a tradition-bucking tradition was born. In the opening ceremonies of the Olympic Games, the American delegation does not lower its flag. The American flag has remained high before kings, presidents and emperors. It has not dipped in deference to such great nations Canada, Germany or China.

No matter the dignitary and no matter the country, in the opening ceremonies of the Olympic Games, the Americans keep their flag standing tall with pride, confidence and optimism ... proud of its past contribution to the world ... confident of its place as a leader in global humanity ... optimistic of its role in a great future.

You are no different from the American flag. You have every reason to stand tall in any situation, no matter whom you encounter. Thus, you should shy away from no one.

Yes, there are people who have accomplished much – award-winning authors, note-worthy business professionals, and civic leaders of every kind. Do not concede anything to them. Rather, stop, reflect, and take inventory of your own past. It is a proud one too – marked by wonderful milestones, accomplishments, and achievements.

Yes, there are people who offer a great deal to society – architects of innovation, masters of a craft, and commanders of loyal followers. Do not wilt in their presence. Rather have every confidence that no matter what you do, your contribution to society serves to make the world a better place – even if it is just in your little corner of it.

Yes, there are people whose crowning achievements are clearly ahead of them – future dignitaries, rising-corporate stars, and budding entrepreneur types. Do not back down from them. No matter how high their stock may rise, remember you should have every optimism that yours will rise too.

In short, no matter where you find yourself and no matter whose company you are in, believe that you belong. As such, stand tall. Throw your shoulders back and freely involve yourself in the world around you. No matter what, do not bow to any earthly king.

Chapter 22
Eleven Seconds To Courage

Life Will Give You Tragedies And Setbacks. Forge Ahead Despite Them.

The sport of hockey is integral to Travis Roy's life. He first put on ice skates at just 20 months old and thus he has been deeply involved in the sport of hockey for as long as he could remember.

The summer before Travis entered the seventh grade, he went to hockey camp. At the camp, one of the counselors suggested that Travis make a list of hockey goals. That he did. He wrote down where he was and where he wanted to be.

Travis' list was an extensive one. Toward the end of the list, he wrote that he wanted to play for an NCAA Division I college, similar to his father who was a Hall of Fame player for the University of Vermont in the mid 1960's.

With the support of his parents, Travis sought the best competition to challenge his hockey skills and achieve his goals. As a result, he transferred to Tabor Academy in Marion, Massachusetts his junior year. While this change would require him to live away from home, this new school would provide him greater exposure to the recruiting efforts of NCAA Division I hockey programs.

The decision to attend Tabor Academy in the end was a wise one. Travis drew interest from several NCAA Division I hockey programs. Ultimately, he chose to attend Boston University, signing a letter of intent and accepting a scholarship to play hockey for the 1995 NCAA National Champion Terriers.

In the fall of 1995, Travis was set to achieve one of his final goals – play NCAA Division I hockey. At 20 years of age, on October 20, 1995, Travis entered into his first collegiate hockey game with less than two minutes having expired in the game.

Immediately after the face-off, Travis chased an opposing player into the corner after a loose puck, something he had done thousands of times before. This time, however, his feet became tangled up as he approached and he fell headlong forward.

All within 11 seconds, Travis' life changed forever. As he crashed into the boards, he cracked his fourth and fifth cervical vertebra. In an instant, he was paralyzed from the neck down.

For Travis Roy this was a tragic setback, one that very few can begin to imagine. At that point, he had a choice: Lead a sad life of anguish and self-pity or, despite his limitations, continue driving himself forward as a high achiever.

In the weeks and months following his injury, he wrestled with that choice. He certainly had difficult days, filled with anger, sorrow, and frustration. It would have been easy for him to follow a sorrowful path. Moreover, few would have faulted him.

Travis, however, did not choose that path. Eventually, he took command of his attitude. In doing so, he replaced fears of the unknown and feelings of self-pity with an attitude of courageous determination.

He engaged in an intense rehabilitation regime in both Boston and Atlanta, allowing him to regain some movement in his right arm. That year he returned to Boston University to become involved with his teammates' quest for another hockey national championship and then began attending class less than a year after his accident.

In 1997, Travis wrote *Eleven Seconds: A Story of Tragedy, Courage & Triumph,* which is now in its sixth printing. This book provides an account of how he realized his dream to play NCAA Division I hockey, how he managed through his paralysis and how he developed a determination to build himself for the future.

Travis graduated in four years from Boston University with a degree in public relations. In addition, Travis has become an articulate advocate for individuals living with spinal cord injuries. He is a frequent speaker on the need for increased medical funding in this area and the hope that continued spinal cord research carries on. This includes testifying before a U.S. Senate Committee hearing for The National Institutes of Health in Washington, D.C. and the Massachusetts state legislature.

He founded and remains actively involved with the Travis Roy Foundation, a 501(c)(3) organization that focuses on finding a cure for spinal cord injuries. This organization also provides grants to spinal cord injury survivors in financial need to help them purchase costly adaptive equipment necessary to live more active and independent lives.

Travis is also a popular motivational speaker. Speaking on topics such as "Conquering Life's Hurdles" and "A Change In Plans," Travis addresses corporate executives as well as school children from around the country on finding meaning and success in spite of the obstacles and setting goals and establishing values to make them come true.

Years after his accident, Travis continues to be a unifying figure, an inspiration for others and a tremendous success. This all has occurred because in the wake of a terrible setback, he demonstrated an attitude of courageous determination. As a result, he draws to himself others who cannot help but want to associate with him.

For us the lesson is simple. Life is not an endless succession of forward progress. You will experience setbacks, disappointments, and even tragedy in your life. Whatever the adversity, you need to forge ahead with great courage and determination.

Remember, there are no awards or accolades for sulking and self-pity. It is courage that will get you noticed. Moreover, it is this strong will that serves to draw people to you and makes them want to associate with you.

Chapter 23
Standing O-H ... I-O

Great People Applaud The Achievements Of Others.

The state of Ohio loves its football, especially the Ohio State Buckeyes. That is a fact. The team reigns supreme in the hearts and minds of most everyone. Ohio State memorabilia flies off the shelves. Families plan their weddings and other notable familial events around Saturdays in the fall, carefully trying to determine if there is a home game or not.

This all may seem odd to a visitor to Columbus, Ohio – a singular fixation on one team. If you live here, however, you would quickly learn about all the rich tradition that is behind this fanatical behavior: Ohio Stadium, better known as The Horseshoe ... Woody Hayes ... Brutus Buckeye ... The Best Damn Band In The Land (aka, TBDBITL) and Script Ohio ... The song Hang on Sloopy ... and this list could go on for pages.

Why is there such a love for the beloved Buckeyes? One could argue that there are few cities in this country with a population of over a million people that are home to a major college with the stature of the Ohio State University, but that do not have a major professional sports franchise to serve as distraction. The reason there is such a love for the Buckeyes is that people love the Buckeyes. There need be no real reason. It just is. And as a result, there are two times of year: football season and the countdown to football season.

If you shout "O-H" in Columbus (or pretty much anywhere in the world for that matter), you can be assured that you will get in return a resounding "I-O." It is like a mantra or means of identification for those in the Buckeye Nation – which is a collective moniker for Ohio State fans worldwide.

The Ohio State Buckeyes football program is arguably a great one. Over the years, this football program has given Buckeye Nation a steady flow of great players for which they can stand and give an ovation. Archie Griffin … Chris Spielman … Eddie George … and, Tom Harmon.

Wait. That's not correct. Tom Harmon played football for the Michigan Wolverines, the hated rival of the Ohio State Buckeyes. There is no way Buckeye Nation would offer any sort of accolades to someone from "that school up north." Nevertheless, they gave him an ovation.

On November 23, 1940, Tom Harmon led the Michigan Wolverines into Ohio Stadium for the final game of his college career. He was a two-way player for the Wolverines and routinely played the entire game for the Maize and Blue. The media touted Harmon as one of the best players in the country and a top candidate to win the 1940 Heisman trophy (as he missed winning it in 1939 by a mere 150 votes).

Those in attendance at Ohio Stadium knew that Harmon had to have a great game to solidify his Heisman candidacy. Harmon did not disappoint over the course of the afternoon. On the offensive side of the ball, he was 11 for 12 in passing for 151 yards and rushed for another 139 yards. Plus, he scored five touchdowns (three running and two passing) and made four extra points. On defense and special teams, he intercepted the ball three times and punted the ball three times for an average of 50 yards. Due in large part to Harmon's efforts, the Wolverines beat the Buckeyes 40-0.

As the final seconds clicked down on Michigan's victory, Buckeye fans rose to their feet and began clapping for Harmon. In an unprecedented display of admiration (not seen before nor since), this quickly grew into a thunderous ovation for Michigan's number 98. Buckeye Nation was certainly not happy about the lopsided defeat, but they could not help but notice and appreciate the great player and his contribution to college football.

In life from time to time, you will happen across someone that has made a remarkable accomplishment. Outstanding academic achievement. A successful marketing campaign. A stellar product or service. A wonderful performance or program. A greener lawn or a more robust garden. Whatever the case, acknowledge and applaud their feat – even if it served to highlight your shortcomings.

Chapter 24
Singles Score Runs Too!

Seemingly Inconsequential Opportunities Are As Important As Great Ones.

Chances are, you played baseball at least once in your life. It may have been just a pick-up game in the street. It may have been a required game in school gym class. It may have only been tee ball. Whatever the case, you played baseball.

Reflect back to the first time you were up to bat. What did you do? Did you attempt to bunt? No. Did you earn a walk to first base on a series of bad pitches? No. What did you do?

You likely tried to hit the ball as hard as you could. Now, you may have struck out in the process. Alternatively, you may have ground out to the shortstop. On the other hand, you may have popped out to left field. Whatever the case, your intent was to whack the ball out of the park and then enjoy a slow meander around the bases.

Unfortunately, this is indicative of how you might approach life. When it comes to looking for opportunities or contacts, we go for the home run ball. That is, you reserve your best effort for those people or situations that are likely to yield some real results – runs or scores, in baseball vernacular.

You might reserve your eye contact for the potential new clients (and perhaps look through those who would never be). You tend not to flash your warm smile unless you can deploy it on those people responsible for hiring and promoting. You ostensibly cannot muster a "how are you doing?" "hello," or even a "hi," unless it is directed at someone of significant consequence to you.

Far too often, you may not want to be bothered with that person who does not appear to have the potential to provide you direct benefit. They might represent getting to first, second or third base, but little more. As a result, your actions reflect your attitude. For these people, you offer no polite pleasantries. You generally maintain a straight face when you encounter them. Moreover, if you have eye contact at all, it is for a fleeting uncomfortable split second.

You should take a lesson from baseball. According to Major League Baseball statistics, if the only way a player could score in baseball was to hit a home run, there would be over 75% fewer runs. In fact, in baseball at any level, runs are largely the result of activities other than home runs. Teams infrequently attempt to score relying on blasts out of the park. Rather, baseball teams score runs by stringing together a series of walks, hits, and stolen bases.

Certainly, home runs are exciting and they are responsible for driving in runs other than just the batter. However, those extra runs batted in are the result of preceding walks, singles, doubles, and triples. In baseball, there is a combination of strategy and luck involved in getting a player safely home. However, no successful baseball team relies entirely on the home run day in and day out. Rather, they look to the seemingly inconsequential plays and strategies to build single game victories (and longer-term successful seasons).

You should follow this strategy in your approach to achieving success, seeking opportunity, or operating in life. Certainly, some things generate immediate results. Absolutely, certain situations hold huge promises here and now. From these you get clients, jobs, and other opportunities. These are the home runs. Just as in baseball, you should rejoice at these accomplishments and celebrate.

The reality is not every opportunity, situation or new contact will generate immediate results or value at all. Value still exists. There is promise in every occasion, circumstance, or person. While not everything creates results in and of itself, every contact serves as something upon which you can build – making for a great day, week, or year.

Some opportunities, situations, or contacts you can deem as singles, some doubles, and still other triples. As such, they may not seem exciting in the moment. Remember, however, they each serve to move you closer to scoring those metaphorical runs.

With any opportunity or situation, approach it as if a million dollars is on the line. In reality, it is. Chances are this one opportunity or situation essentially builds towards something substantial.

Home runs – in life or with personal contacts – are great. Often they make your day, year, or even life. All the same, despite the attraction of realizing these moments of celebration, you need to keep in mind that singles score runs too.

Chapter 25
Bonnie Richardson High

Sometimes, It's Just Up To You.

In 2009, Rochelle High School won the Texas Class 1A high school girls track championship. That, in and of itself, is not remarkable – some high school wins the girls track and field state championship every year. The remarkable thing about this state championship, however, is that the Rochelle Hornets won it the year before as well.

The even more remarkable thing about the back-to-back state titles, however, is that the high school does not even have a track to practice on. Located almost in the dead center of Texas (about 140 miles northeast of Austin), Rochelle is a small, unincorporated farming community with modest means. About once a year, the McCulloch County commissioner will smooth out a circular path of hard, rutted caliche – a layer of soil in which the soil particles have been cemented together by lime.

Perhaps the most remarkable thing about the back-to-back titles for the track team with no track on which to practice is that one girl was responsible for both state championships – Bonnie Richardson.

Track is a team sport comprised of various individual events (and a handful of four-person relays). While participants (or four-person relays) compete for individual placing within a particular event, this placement generates team points for the respective school the individual person (or relay team) represents.

Thus, a high school would accumulate, for example, ten points if one of its athletes finished first, eight for second, six for third, etc. These points are then aggregated for each high school. The high school whose athletes generate the most total points at the state meet is declared the state championship.

In 2008, Bonnie Richardson was the only girl from Rochelle High School to qualify for the state meet. That did not matter. At the first day of the meet, she won the high jump (5 feet, 5 inches), placed second in the long jump (18 feet, 7 inches) and finished third in the discus (121 feet even).

On the second day, she won the 200 meters (25.03 seconds) and took second in the 100 meters (12.19 seconds), almost upsetting the defending state champion in the event. When the meet officials tallied the points for those finishes, Bonnie Richardson, the daughter of a Rochelle High School teacher and rancher, tallied 42 team points.

This was six points more than Chilton High School. Thus the Rochelle Hornets were the Class 1A state champions. According to the University Interscholastic League, the state's high school sports governing body, Richardson was the first girl and second athlete (since 1970 when Meridian High School, Baylor Bear, and Pittsburgh Steelers Frank Pollard did it) to accomplish winning a state track title singlehandedly.

In 2009, the valedictorian of her 14-student senior class, repeated her previous year feat, defeating 56 other schools. In five events, she won four medals (gold in the long jump and high jump; silver in the discus, and bronze in the 200 meters) and took fourth in the 100 meter run.

Certainly, track is largely an individual sport. A high school state championship, however, is a team endeavor. While Richardson was part of the team, winning a state title was on her.

Life in many respects is much like a team track championship. Success relies on achievement of many individual activities. These individual activities then coalesce into an overall team effort.

Like Richardson's back-to-back track state championships for Rochelle High School, sometimes the support is not there. In those situations, if it is going to happen, it is entirely up to you. It does no good to lament your situation. You just need to rise up, do your best, and try to make it happen.

Chapter 26
A Perfect Shame

Don't Live By Others' Recognition Of Your Achievements.

Many consider the greatest game ever pitched to be Don Larsen's perfect game in the 1956 World Series. They could be right, as this occurred on baseball's biggest stage. Arguably, however, the greatest game ever pitched occurred a few short years after that.

On May 26, 1959, the Milwaukee Braves were hosting the Pittsburg Pirates with 19,154 fans in County Stadium. The evening was dark with the constant threat of storms. Off in the distance there were jagged bolts of lightning and rain. This resulted in gusty winds at the ballpark.

Despite the dramatic weather, there was nothing overly remarkable about this contest. It was a regularly scheduled game in a long list of regular season games for both teams. Essentially, it was just another evening baseball game.

As it was just another game, the Pirates followed its normal pitching rotation. As such, slated to start was 5-foot-9, 155 pound, 33-year-old Harvey Haddix. Growing up in Clark County, Ohio, about an hour west of Columbus, he developed his physical prowess working on the family farm.

This evening, however, Haddix would need all his farmyard development, as this game was not a typical assignment. The Milwaukee Braves had won two consecutive National League pennants. Additionally, 38 games into the season, the defending pennant champions had five players who were hitting better than .300. One of those batters was Hank Aaron, who at the time had an incredible .453 average.

Despite the difficulty of the assignment, Haddix got after it in the bottom of the first inning. Fighting a cold, he recorded an out on his first pitch. The second batter, however, took him to a full count before lining out. Hank Aaron, the third batter, hit a pop fly that a Pirate fielder easily caught. Three up. Three down. Haddix retired the side.

The first inning was foretelling of Haddix's effort that evening. Batter after batter, he recorded an out. While he earned only eight strikeouts, the field-play outs Pittsburgh recorded were also a result of great pitching. No one in the Milwaukee Brave line up could effectively hit the "fastball, sharp slider, or deceptive curve," that Haddix routinely delivered with pinpoint control.

In the ninth inning, Haddix recorded his eighth strikeout – interestingly enough against Milwaukee's pitcher. The home crowd – which included a young Bud Selig – rose to their feet, applauding the Pirate pitcher. After nine innings and 27 batters, no Brave had made it to base – not on a hit ... not on a walk ... not even on an error. Haddix was perfect.

The problem was that after nine innings, the Pittsburgh Pirates had not scored a run. Unfortunately, two of their future MVP's were not in the lineup due to various reasons. Despite this, they had more than their share of chances. Pittsburgh batters were very productive. Against Milwaukee's starting pitcher, Lew Burdette, the Pirates recorded 12 hits in nine innings of play – one was by Haddix himself.

The Pirates had runners in scoring position. In the second inning, they recorded three singles. However, they did not score, as a base runner was thrown out trying to make it to third. Other opportunities the Braves foiled, recording three timely double plays. Furthermore, they committed no errors.

Brave pitcher Burdette did his part as well. While he only recorded two strikes outs, he did not walk a single Pirate batter. If Pittsburgh was going to score, they would have to earn it.

In fact, in the top of the seventh they nearly did. Pittsburgh's Bob Skinner connected with the ball. Smack! Everyone expected it to head over the wall. Fortunately, however, Mother Nature played her part in the pitching drama. A gust of wind damped the balls momentum, keeping it in play. Hank Aaron caught the ball at the wall. The game was destined to go to extra innings.

Haddix continued to pitch. Moreover, he continued to pitch remarkably. In inning 10, three up, three down. He repeated that in inning 11. Then, he did it again in inning 12.

In the bottom of the 13th, however, the first batter for the Braves connected with the ball. Like so many other for s throughout the game, the ball gently bounded towards the waiting glove of Pirate third baseman Don Hoak. He cleanly fielded the ball, but over threw first base. The batter took first base.

The next Milwaukee batter executed a textbook sacrifice. Intentionally, he bunted the ball so that the only play the Pirates had was to throw him out at first. This, however, allowed the Brave on first to advance to second. Milwaukee had a runner in scoring position.

Next at bat was Hank Aaron. Pittsburgh did not want to take a chance. Haddix followed the directive of his manager and intentionally walked the home run king.

The next Brave batter was not much better – Joe Adcock, a dangerous right-handed power hitter. Nevertheless, Haddix was determined to get back on track. He dug in and fired the first pitch.

"Ball," the umpire declared.

On the next pitch, Adcock pounded the ball to deep right center field. It cut through the wind and sailed over the bullpen for the apparent game winner.

The runner on second rounded third and crossed home plate. Believing that the game was over, Hank Aaron trotted off, cutting across the field – never touching third base or home plate. Adcock, however, took his slow meander around the bases.

As Aaron had left the baselines, he was out. As Adcock had advanced ahead of Aaron, the umpires declared him out as well. Adcock received credit for only a double. Despite the base running blunder, the damage was done. The game was over. The official score was Milwaukee Braves 1, Pittsburgh Pirates 0.

Despite the outcome, almost everyone who attended or listened to the game proclaim it "the best game ever pitched." Further, Major League Baseball (MLB), the media, and baseball fans deemed that Haddix pitched a perfect game. Nevertheless, MLB credited him with the loss.

Most agree that pinning the loss on Haddix was a shame. Pittsburgh Pirate fans declared it a shame. The media declared it a shame. Baseball fans everywhere – including Milwaukee Braves fans – declared it a shame. Even Lew Burdette, Haddix's opposing pitcher, declared it a shame. Nevertheless, those are baseball rules: one is the winning pitcher and another is the losing.

Exacerbating the indignity, in 1991 the MLB Committee for Statistical Accuracy in Baseball revoked the game's "perfect" status. Chaired by Commissioner Fay Vincent, the Committee announced that it did not meet the "perfect game" criteria because Harry Haddix lost.

While pinning the loss on Haddix and changing the classification of his remarkable pitching effort were a shame, neither of these things changed the underlying achievement. In 12 and two-third innings, Harry Haddix faced only 40 batters and gave up only one hit. During the first nine innings, he did not give up a hit or a walk and none of the 27 batters he faced got on base. Despite the changing classification, it was a perfect game. Despite crediting Haddix with the loss, he had a remarkable pitching performance. Whatever the case, it is arguably the greatest game ever pitched.

While you might not be a major league pitcher, no doubt you have had wonderful achievements. Further, no doubt your great achievements may have been lost to an overall dismal performance. Or perhaps it was the blunder of someone else that cast a dark shadow on your accomplishment. Or perhaps a fluke circumstance or misclassification will serve to take some of the luster off an otherwise shining moment.

Whatever the case, remember the achievement is still there. You still have reason to feel proud (even though you might not openly celebrate). Your hard work and dedication still had meaning. Remember, your achievements and accomplishments are yours. They do not depend upon the recognition of others.

Chapter 27
The Fiesta Fake Out

*Work Hard And Sacrifice;
Someone Will Notice.*

On January 3, 2013, Dane Ebanez did something that few football players ever have the opportunity to do. He played football in a college bowl game.

Think about it. Millions of boys and girls play football in a Pop Warner or flag league. Of those, only tens of thousands go on to play high school football. From there only a small percentage of high school football players go on to play football in college.

College football in the United States has a handful of sanctioning organizations, but only one has a bowl system – the National Collegiate Athletic Association (NCAA). Within the NCAA, however, there are different levels of competition – Division I, Division II, Division III – and not every level competes in bowls. Only those football teams who are part of the NCAA Division I Bowl Subdivision are eligible to compete in a bowl game.

Even amongst the Division I Bowl Subdivision ranks, however, not every team is fortunate enough to be invited to play in a bowl game. This is limited to only those teams with a solid winning record. As many teams finish their regular season with more losses than wins, the number of NCAA teams making it to a bowl game is small.

Of those football teams that get the privilege of being invited to a college bowl game, not everyone will see game action. A NCAA Division I football team may have over 100 players amongst its ranks. Only a few dozen are starters or play on special teams.

As such, many players on bowl teams have virtually no chance of seeing game action. They simply have some of the best seats in the house for a nationally televised bowl. Thus, when Dane Ebanez, who was participating in his final game as an Oregon Duck football player, stepped onto the field in the Fiesta Bowl, it was quite an accomplishment and the thrill of a lifetime for him.

It is important to note, Dane was not a superstar for the Ducks. No one was scrambling to get a replica number 91 jersey with the name "Ebanez" emblazed across the back. There were no NFL scouts keenly watching him from some obscure luxury box.

He was not even a starter. Playing wide receiver, Dane was in line behind a deep stable of other "more capable" players. After all, he only stood 5'9" tall and weighed a modest 180 pounds. Dane was technically not even a back-up player. Nevertheless, he made an actual game appearance in the 2013 Fiesta Bowl.

This was somewhat of a milestone, considering the odds were long that Dane would be part of any college football program. He came to the University of Oregon from North Pole, Alaska, hardly a football hotbed. Besides, Dane played soccer in high school.

When he arrived on campus his first year, however, the Oregon football team was conducting open tryouts. The coaching staff was hopeful of finding some undiscovered football talent roaming the campus.

The odds of this are small. Nevertheless, through his work ethic and athletic ability, the coaching staff noticed Dane. They invited him to be part of the scout team as a walk-on.

What this meant is that Dane's role, along with other scout players, would be to mimic the upcoming opponents' offense or defense. This required him to be involved in all the trappings of major college football – practice, film sessions, and conditioning.

As a walk-on, however, Dane would not get financial assistance. In fact, he got nothing for the hours he devoted to the Oregon football program, not even a meal. Moreover, because of all the time learning opposition plays, practice and conditioning, he was unable to hold a part-time job. This meant that over four years he had to take out more than $70,000 in student loans to fund tuition and fees, room and board, and books and supplies.

Despite the seemingly inequitable circumstances, Dane took his role seriously. He never missed practice, always worked hard, and did whatever the coaches asked. He prided himself on being an effective scout player. In fact, over his tenure as a scout player for the Oregon Ducks, the team named him in consecutive years the scout team's offensive player of the year, the defensive scout team player of the year, and the scout team special team player of the year.

Despite all of this, it was unlikely that he would see any game action in the Fiesta Bowl. Yet he did. It, however, was not the function of the coaching staff working him into the plan. They were far too consumed with bowl game preparation to concern themselves as to whether a scout player gets field time – even one with Dane's scout team credentials.

Nevertheless, it mattered to someone that Dane Ebanez get his due. With 2:30 left in the Fiesta Bowl, the Ducks had just scored extending its lead to 35-17. Following normal team celebrations, the kick-off team took the field and huddled.

As the huddle broke, Oregon players scurried to their positions, including sophomore Keanon Lowe. He was a player on scholarship. As a back-up wide receiver, he had made 22 catches and scored three touchdowns. His main role for the Ducks this season, however, was on special teams.

As a starter on special teams, Lowe had a back-up – Dane Ebanez. He certainly knew his back-up. Moreover, he bore witness to Dane's hard work and sacrifice. He also understood how special it would be to say that he played in the Fiesta Bowl.

With all this, Lowe had plotted to get Dane on the field. As he trotted towards his position on the field, Lowe feigned an injury. He motioned to the special team coaches. They immediately motioned to Dane – the hard working, self-sacrificing scout team player – to hurry onto the field for a single play in the 2013 Fiesta Bowl.

Work hard. Someone will see it. Sacrifice. Someone will know. There is no guarantee that someone will reward the effort. Nevertheless, do not be afraid to work hard and sacrifice. It will not go unnoticed.

Chapter 28
One For Dad

Little Things In Your Hands, Can Be Immense In The Hands Of Another.

With six minutes remaining in the fourth quarter, the St. Clairsville High School football team had a 20-plus point lead over its host, the Wildcats of Richmond Edison High School. Despite the commanding lead, the Red Devils were not done. They intended to score one more touchdown.

The need for one more score was not about breaking the 50-point mark. It had nothing to do school records. It was not about "padding stats" for the Ohio High School Athletic Associations (OHSAA) complicated selection process for football playoff bids.

With unfinished business in mind, the Red Devil quarterback set the play in motion as he had done a few dozen times before on this early October Friday evening. While they were intent on scoring, it was merely just a hope at this point – the line of scrimmage was almost 60 yards from the end zone.

Nevertheless, the quarterback received the snap from center, took a step back, and handed the ball off to one of the team's running backs. There were no plans to run out the clock. The direction was clearly forward towards "pay dirt."

As the offensive line surged forward – moving defenders much like it had been doing all game – it created a seam. The Red Devil running back instinctively found it, quickly changed direction, and darted towards the open field. It was easy to see the number of the player carrying the football.

Number 10 was Michael Ferns. In mere seconds, his back was through the line of scrimmage and across midfield. No one on the Wildcats defense even seemed to make contact with him.

Ferns accelerated forward as if this particular play mattered more than any other did. He had not even reached the Richmond Edison 40-yard line when he seemed to be running alone on the field. The defenders behind him were losing ground and the defenders down field simply did not have the right angles to make a play.

Ferns lengthened his stride, as he passed the 35. He continued to churn his arms. He crossed the 30 and then the 25. This would be his 12th touchdown of the season.

Ferns pushed on. Crossing the 20, he angled towards the front end zone pylon. There would likely be much more, he was only a junior. Moreover, he was a starter on an undefeated Red Devils team that many projected to make a deep run into the OHSAA Division IV playoffs.

He continued, rolling over the 15 and then two-and-half strides later the 10. Beyond his high school career, Ferns had already committed to play football at the University of Michigan. There was no doubt he was a great football player and there was much more glory for him ahead, starting with the end zone five yards away.

On this night, on this play, no one was going to stop Michael Ferns from scoring. No one. No one, except Michael Ferns.

Just before Ferns crossed into the end zone, he deliberately stepped out of bounds. The cheering and elation amongst the St. Clairsville faithful, immediately shifted to confusion. Their mumbles in the bleachers were best summarized as, "Huh? What? Why?"

Even the officials were perplexed. Two signaled touchdown. Immediately, however, Michael Ferns and a few of his teammates adamantly argued against their own achievement. The officials uncharacteristically reversed themselves and waved off the touchdown.

The officials still did not understand. Nevertheless, they set the line of scrimmage short of the end zone, and signaled the officials working the chains to indicate first down. Quickly, the scoreboard mimicked the down-and-distance situation.

Family and friends from both fan bases looked to one another for answers. The situation was inexplicable. Nevertheless, the game continued and the Wildcat defense – not knowing why – nevertheless prepared for a goal line stand.

While almost everyone was confused, there were those who understood clearly. One was St. Clairsville coach Brett McLean. Before Ferns had even stepped out of bounds, he began shouting on the sidelines, "Thompson, Thompson, Thompson." He was calling for Logan Thompson.

Coach McLean caught Logan Thompson off guard. Like most Red Devil players, he was caught up in the excitement of Michael Ferns' run. Nevertheless, Thompson complied and found himself standing next to the Red Devil head coach, but not understanding why.

"You're going in at running back," McLean yelled. "Tell them to run 26 Power."

Thompson was stunned. As a freshman on one of the best football teams in the state, he had no expectation of playing. As a linebacker and occasional wide receiver, he was completely out of his element.

Sensing his freshman's uneasiness, McLean continued, "It's easy. Just follow Michael Ferns' big butt."

As Logan Thompson took to the field, the Red Devil freshman only exacerbated the confusion rippling through the stadium. "Who is number 17? Was Michael Ferns hurt? What is Coach McLean doing?" The coach, however, knew exactly what he was doing.

Thirty-six hours earlier, life forced Logan Thompson to grow beyond his 15 years. He found himself using a baseball bat to tear through a wooden door. Moments earlier, his mother had heard Logan's father collapse in the bathroom. As his father was unresponsive to his wife and kids, Logan jumped into action. His violent rampage was a desperate attempt to help his father.

On October 3, 2012, emergency responders rushed 44-year-old Paul Thompson to the hospital. He had suffered a stroke. Despite Logan's valiant effort, however, his father died at the hospital.

When Logan's mother, Daniele returned from the hospital, she shared the terrible news with her three boys, Logan, Landen, and Lancen. While tears and sorrow consumed them, Logan made the decision that he wanted to go to school. He was looking for relief from what had just happened.

At school, Logan sought out Coach McLean and informed him, "My dad is dead. He died this morning." Stunned, the coach reflectively asked, "What are you doing here?"

While word of Paul Thompson's tragic death spread throughout the school, the day was as normal as it could be for Logan. He attended algebra, U.S. history and every other class. When the day was over, he did what he did everyday: He went to football practice.

His coaches and teammates were perplexed by Logan's behavior. They could not imagine what Logan was feeling. Nevertheless, they wanted to be there for him however they could. Coach McLean again asked, "What are you doing here?"

At practice, Logan informed the coaching staff that he would be there the following night. Like every Friday night, he intended to be on the bus for the team's away game in Richmond, Ohio. Just like every other freshman and reserve player, he was going to be on the sidelines, in uniform, supporting the varsity team.

Coach McLean attempted to talk Logan out of his decision. "Stay at home. Grieve for your father. Support your mother. Why come to the game? It is not that important."

Logan would not relent, reasoning, "If my dad were still here, he would've wanted me to go. And even though he's not here, he'd want me to go. He wouldn't want me missing out." He spoke as if attending the game were in some way a tribute to his recently deceased father – even if his contribution was limited to being on the sidelines.

Being on the sidelines for all four quarters, however, was not part of the game plan. After learning of Logan's loss, his commitment to the team, and tribute to his father, the coaching staff and team leaders wanted to do something special for Logan.

Thus, Michael Ferns' actions were hardly inexplicable to those in the know. They were part of the plan. Michael Ferns was well aware of what he was doing. He was merely surrendering what would have been just another touchdown in a litany of touchdowns over a football career. In surrendering it, he was hopeful it would have tremendous significance in the hands of another.

On the next play, the St. Clairsville Red Devils executed 26 Power just as they had done so dozens of times before in practice. On the next play, Logan Thompson executed 26 Power just as Coach McLean had instructed him. He followed Michael Ferns into the end zone, completing the game plan, and making a touchdown tribute to this father.

No doubt, life has blessed you with something. It might be wealth, a special talent, or an incredible network. Whatever it is, find the selflessness to share a piece of it, just as Michael Ferns and the Red Devil coaching staff sought to share a bit of glory. While that small piece may be insignificant in your hands, the value of it may well be immense in the hands of another.

Chapter 29
Harvard Beats Yale 29-29

Don't Buy Into The Hype Of Others.

There was a time when Ivy League football mattered. Before NCAA Division I college football became big business, Ivy League schools were all somehow factors. In discussing the national championship picture, the media bantered about names like Cornell, Harvard and Yale with the likes of Notre Dame, Ohio State and Alabama. In fact, between Harvard and Yale the schools accounted for 25 national titles.

The end of the Ivy League's prowess on the national championship stage was in 1968. That year, the media touted the Yale Bulldogs as not just a sure bet to win the Ivy League conference, but also ranked them near the top of the Associated Press polls.

Driving the Bulldogs national prominence was its seemingly unstoppable star-laden offense. Amongst its litany of stars was quarterback Brian Dowling, who had led Yale to 16 straight wins and had not lost a game since the sixth grade. Aiding Dowling was his "go-to" player, Calvin Hill – a future NFL rookie of the year and Dallas Cowboy star.

Together, Dowling and Hill (along with a litany of other college notables) tore through its non-conference and Ivy League schedule. The Bulldogs had done so in a convincing fashion, averaging 36 points per game, which was one of the best averages in the country. The only thing between them, an Ivy League title, and a perfect season was rival Harvard University.

Harvard, however, had no standouts, no football stars, and certainly no future professional players. As such, the media and conference coaches had few positive accolades for the Crimson. In fact, many expected them to finish last in the Ivy League Conference. This prediction appeared dead on in their first game, as they were only able to squeak out a 27-20 win against lower-division Holy Cross.

As the season rolled on, however, Harvard improved, surprising many. Even more surprising, it managed to stay undefeated. While they lacked star power, the team was a hardnosed group. This made for a stingy defense, which had allowed only seven points per game on average.

Despite this incredible defense and being undefeated, few gave Harvard any chance against mighty Yale. After all, the Crimson had barely beaten a NCAA Division I-AA team. While they had a staunch defense, their offense was suspect. Moreover, the Yale Bulldogs were a star-laden, offensive juggernaut.

Harvard did not care. It did not matter what the world of armchair quarterbacks predicted, Yale would have to prove it on the field. Thus, on November 23, 1968 before 57,750 fans at Harvard Stadium the Crimson kicked off to its Ivy League rivals.

Unfortunately, things did not start well for Harvard. Yale's Dowling ran for a touchdown, and then he threw to Hill for a second one. After a second Dowling scoring pass, midway through the second quarter, Harvard found itself down by 22, which was more points than it had allowed to any opponent all season.

At this point, those who speculated that Yale would lay a crushing defeat on Harvard likely became smug about their prediction. In their minds, the game was essentially over.

It did not matter, however, what was in the head of those in the stands. What did matter was what the Crimson players felt. They did not intend to concede defeat just yet.

The Harvard defense tightened up. Moreover, the Crimson offense found some life. Just before halftime, they scored. Going into the locker room at halftime, they only trailed 22-6.

Nevertheless, those believing they knew better declared that there was no way Harvard could come back from such a deficit against Yale. They asserted that the Bulldogs still had points to score and there was no way the Crimson could keep pace.

The problem with these predictions was that someone failed to tell the Harvard team. Or it might have been that they did and that the Crimson were just not listening. After all, they sensed some momentum heading into the locker room at the half. They intended to capitalize on it.

Harvard received the opening kickoff in the second half ready to make a case for a comeback. They were unable, however. After only three plays, Yale forced them to punt the ball back. It appeared as if the possibility of a comeback was short-lived.

The Crimson players were not willing to go away. They did not care what the media was saying and ignored what so-called experts might have thought. They were not willing to kowtow to the Yale Bulldog "star power" hype.

This mindset served them well. While Harvard punted the football back to Yale, the Bulldogs did not have it long. Someone on that star-laden Yale team fumbled and players from both sides scrambled for the ball. On this miscue, unheralded Harvard managed to not just recover the football, but also do so in the Yale end zone. An extra point later, the Crimson was now only down 22-13.

"Fluke play. No way this changes the final result," onlookers thought. After all, it was the stars from Yale versus the nobodies from Harvard.

For the balance of the third quarter and on into the fourth, these thoughts would seem to prevail. At the beginning of the fourth quarter, Dowling marched his team down the field and ran into the end zone himself for his fourth touchdown.

Yale now led 29-13.

Yale fans taunted those from Harvard. Across the stadium, hundreds of Bulldogs faithfully waved white handkerchiefs in a mockery of its Ivy League rivals. To them, the game was over.

While the game was well in hand, to the Yale offense it was not over. After another defensive stop, Dowling began marching the offense down for another score. It appeared that Yale wanted to not just defeat but to humiliate the Crimson.

As Yale started driving down the field, many Harvard fans moved towards exits. They were anxious to drown their sorrows at a local bar. As they left, they likely thought, "No way our team comes back against the star-powered Bulldogs."

It did not matter what they thought, however. What mattered was what the Harvard players thought, and they still were not ready to concede.

As luck would have it, 14 yards away from a fifth touchdown, the Yale fullback fumbled. Harvard took advantage of this opportunity. While the Crimson trailed by 16 points they only had 3:34 remaining in the game. They now had the ball, however. In their minds, they still had a chance.

Now relying on their backup quarterback, Harvard began to methodically drive down field. There appeared to be life to a comeback, at least for the time being.

With a third down and 18 on the Yale 38, the Bulldogs managed to get to the quarterback. In addition to pulling Harvard's QB to the ground, they forced him to fumble. This seemed to douse Harvard's momentum.

This let down, however, only lasted momentarily. As luck would have it, the ball dribbled out of quarterback's arms and into the hands of Fritz Reed, Harvard lineman. Seizing the opportunity, Reed lumbered to the Yale 15 before frantic Bulldogs could get him to the ground.

There was still life to the comeback. Two passes later, Harvard scored. With six more points, they now trailed 29-19 with 42 seconds left in the game. They needed a two-point conversion to have even a slim chance.

Unfortunately, the Crimson failed a pass attempt. "Oh well. We gave it a valiant effort," those remaining Harvard fans likely thought.

It did not matter what the fans thought, however. The Harvard team hung onto every hope. And hope came. The officials penalized Yale for pass interference. Harvard had another chance at the conversion, this time a tad closer to the end zone.

The Crimson took advantage of the opportunity. The team's fullback rumbled in for the two desperately needed points. With less than a minute, it was an eight-point game – 29-21.

"Certainly, Yale will hang on," those who originally favored the Bulldogs thought, or at least hoped. After all, in their opinion Yale was man for man the better team.

The Harvard players did not share that opinion. Yale needed to prove it to them. Moreover, they were not going to make it easy. The Crimson lined up for an onside kick.

"The odds do not favor recovering it against the star-laden Bulldogs," detractors rationalized.

The odds of recovery become much more favorable, however, when a team believes. Harvard did. They believed and they recovered the football.

"No way Yale allows the hapless Harvard offense to drive the better part of half the field with less than 40 seconds remaining," cynics sneered.

They did, however. Harvard did not see themselves as inferior. They drove the football to the eight-yard line with three seconds to spare. Then on the final play, the Crimson quarterback took the snap, scrambled, and then, throwing off the wrong foot, he connected with a back in the end zone.

No time remained. Yale led 29-27. Nevertheless, football rules allowed Harvard to attempt a conversion. And they would. After all, they had come this far.

"Certainly, the Yale Bulldogs, with all the accomplished talent, could stop Harvard on this one play," critics quietly lamented.

Not today, however. The credentials that Yale carried into the game certainly did not intimidate Harvard players. At this one moment, it was simply 11 men versus 11 men. Talent and prior accomplishment did not matter. It was down to sheer will.

The Harvard quarterback hit his receiver in the end zone. They had completed the comeback. Scoring 16 points in 42 seconds against a talent-laden, high-powered team, they shared the Ivy League championship with Yale.

Across the front page of the *Crimson* – the Harvard student newspaper – the banner headline fittingly indicated: *"Harvard Beats Yale 29-29."*

In life, you are going to find yourself pitted against what others proclaim as star-laden talent, in the form of business icons, community leaders, and accomplished men and women. So what? They still need to perform under similar circumstances just like you.

In life, you will find that there are those who will be projecting against you. So what? What others predict is in no way definitive (and more than likely unreliable speculation).

In life, do not buy into the hype of other people. If they are going to beat you – in whatever – make them earn it. You should concede nothing.

Chapter 30
Responsible Winning

*Be Of The Same Character In Victory,
As In Defeat.*

Outside of, perhaps soccer, in most every game there is a winner and a loser. Some losses are hard fought battles where it is a shame that either team or player needs to be on the losing end. Some losses are one-sided affairs where the competition completely outmatched the losing team or the losing team experienced an off game.

Then occasionally, a loss is emblematic of a game that the teams should have never played. An example of such a game occurred on January 13, 2009. That evening in Texas high school girls' basketball the Covenant School defeated the Dallas Academy 100 to nothing.

You can derive meaning from this final score. The 100 is obvious – the Covenant School scored early and often. The nothing, however, had two meanings. The first is the apparent one – the Dallas Academy did not score any points. The second is that nothing was gained from this game.

Certainly, the Dallas Academy felt a sense of embarrassment. After a scoreless first quarter, players, coaches and fans probably rationalized to themselves, "This drought won't continue." After a scoreless half, they likely thought, "What are the chances this continues?" After three quarters of scoreless basketball, they no doubt commiserated, "No, this is not happening."

The Covenant School, however, endured a different sort of embarrassment, as they had to justify their actions. Certainly, parents and administrators pondered, "Where is the life lesson here for the kids?" The school had to address the media and public outcry of, "What were you thinking?"

For neutral spectators, there was no entertainment value. For fans of the Dallas Academy, the loss was likely gut wrenching to watch or even learn about. For fans of the Covenant School, there was no real satisfaction.

All that comes from the Covenant School's 100 to nothing drubbing of the Dallas Academy is that there is a certain responsibility to winning. It is not a profound revelation to state that there is no great joy in losing, whether the score is 1-0 or 100-0. It is generally a humbling experience, often described as painful disappointment.

This painful disappointment, however, fuels the euphoria of winning. The very real potential of feeling this pain makes athletes want to celebrate jubilantly when they win. Whatever the sport, however, athletes need to remember that the world respects a modest winner as much as it does someone who loses with a demonstration of great sportsmanship.

This is not to say that winners should not be happy and proud of their accomplishments – they should. Nevertheless, as with all things there are limits to the amount and manner as to how athletes should take their victories. After all, running up the score, celebrating excessively, and gloating does as much (if not more) damage to how others perceive the victor as when they display a miserable disposition in the face of a setback.

Here are five thoughts on responsible winning:

Have Perspective: Put the victory in perspective. While it serves to advance the winner, from an overall perspective it is likely small.

Appreciate The Past: Each win is a culmination of lots of other accomplishments along the way – hard training, game preparation, and successful execution. Without these lesser achievements, the current victory would likely not exist. A responsible winner takes a moment to reflect and appreciate these.

Feel The Pain: Whenever the final score produces a victor, there is someone else on the other end. A responsible winner will reflect on their feelings (and remember that there is no joy in losing) and have a modicum of compassion for them. After all, at one day that might be them.

Move Forward: Remind yourself that just as your failure is not fatal, one win does not give you ultimate success. All that winning generally gives you is the opportunity to work at a higher level. As such, quickly resolve that you need to continue the pursuit of your goals. Otherwise, you run the risk of failing at a higher level.

Look For The Lesson: Every experience offers a lesson. With winning, however, it is not so easy to find these lessons simply because you tend to wrap yourself up in the euphoria of the moment. Nevertheless, quietly consider what you learned from the victory. This will help you temper your celebration and will allow you to earn more accomplishments in the future.

By working through each of these five thoughts, athletes at any level can appropriately temper their victorious euphoria. While they might impress others with on-field triumph, others will appreciate the humble nature with which they achieve them.

While exhibiting responsible winning is an important trait for any athlete, it is not limited to games played on fields, courts, and courses. After all, what is sport? It is simply athletic competition. Absent the athletics, it is merely competition.

As a human being, you compete every day, do you not? In your career, you compete to find a job, get a raise, and obtain a promotion. In business, you compete to obtain an edge so that you can get (and then keep) customers or clients as well as have great employees. At home, you compete to have the nicer house or greener yard and to allow your kids to have the best possible opportunities. The entire human existence – like it or not – is about competing.

Any time there is competition (which is all the time), there are winners and losers ... there is jubilation and frustration ... there is achievement and disappointment. Given that, responsible winning is something you should never stop practicing, no matter how long ago the game passed you by.

Chapter 31
Heroic Assistance

A Loss Is Only A Loss.
It Is Not Failure.

Late in the 2008 softball season, the teams for both Central Washington University and Western Oregon University were in unfamiliar territory. For the first time ever, each had a legitimate chance of making the NCAA Division II tournament, as the two were neck-and-neck atop the Great Northwest Athletic Conference.

Adding to the drama, the Central Washington Wildcats were hosting the Western Oregon Wolves for a conference game at its 300-seat stadium in Ellensburg, 100 miles southeast of Seattle over mountain terrain. The winner would likely clinch the GNAC title and earn a berth. For the loser, the season would be over and for the seniors it would mark the end of a collegiate softball career.

With the game tied 0-0 in the top of the second inning and two runners on base, the Wolves sent to the plate Sara Tucholsky. There was little concern amongst Wildcats players and fans, however. In her four years at Western Oregon, Tucholsky had never hit a collegiate home run. In fact, in her senior campaign she had only tallied three hits in 34 attempts that season. Moreover, Western Oregon's senior was only five feet, two inches tall.

As she readied for the first pitch, Central Washington fans heckled her. Tucholsky tuned it out and watched the first pitch arrive at the plate.

"Strike," the umpire called, causing the heckling to intensify.

Tucholsky did not intend to watch the next pitch. When it arrived, she swung. Not only did she swing, but she also connected and connected well. The ball soared, high and long. Surprising herself, her teammates, and everyone present, the softball flew over the center-field fence.

The Western Oregon bench erupted. The Wolves players raced towards home plate. Courtesy of Tucholsky's heroic shot, they raced to greet their teammates who rounded the bases and headed for home in a careful manner.

Base runner number one crossed home plate to celebration. One run. Soon thereafter, base runner number two crossed home plate to the same. Two runs. The expectation was for three runs, however. Something was wrong.

In her excitement, as Tucholsky began to round the bases, she missed touching first base, a requirement for the home run to count. Realizing her mistake, she stopped and began to double back. At that moment, however, her right knee gave out and she suffered what would prove to be serious ligament damage. The senior went to the ground in agony.

She could not continue. She lay between first and second base. With no ability to advance herself in either direction, Western Oregon coaches had only two options.

They could direct Tucholsky's teammates to help her. The moment they did, however, the umpires had no choice but to declare her out. In this case, the official statistics would not give her credit for the home run.

Western Oregon coaches also had the option of replacing Tucholsky at first base with a pinch runner. This, however, would nullify the senior's home run feat. Rather the official statistics would reflect that Tucholsky's over-the-fence blast was merely a two-run single.

While Western Oregon had only two options, there was a third. "Excuse me. Would it be okay if we carried her around and she touched each bag?" asked Mallory Holtman, a Central Washington player who was motioning towards a teammate as she inquired.

Holtman was a standout for the Wildcats, holding about every major offensive record at Central Washington. As a senior, she had more than her share of home runs and was compassionate towards knee problems as she was contending with her own at the time.

After a brief contemplation, the umpire confirmed that there was nothing in the rulebook preventing Central Washington players from assisting Tucholsky around the bases. With that, Holtman and her shortstop, Liz Wallace, scooped up the fallen Wolves player. They then systematically carried their opponent from first base to second to third and on to home plate, stopping briefly at each base to lower the tiny 5' 2" Tucholsky low enough to tag the base.

This heroic assistance gave the visiting Western Oregon Wolves a 3-0 lead and gave Sara Tucholsky her first and only official collegiate home run. In the end, it cost Central Washington the game, as they were only able to muster two runs throughout the balance of the game. With that, the season was over for the Wildcats and Mallory Holtman had played her last collegiate game.

Despite the heavy cost of their heroic assistance, Holtman and Wallace had no regrets. Finding a victory in the arms of defeat, Holtman shared, "It showed the character of our team ... it shows what our program is about and the kind of people we have here."

In addition to her positive outlook on the events of the Western Oregon season finale, the national media gave significant praise to Wallace and Holtman for their sportsmanship. In the end, the pair were recognized at the AT&T National Sportsmanship Awards. In addition, they won an ESPN ESPY, garnering more votes than Boston Red Sox pitcher Jon Lester (who less than a year after surviving cancer, threw a no-hitter against the Kansas City Royals) and Danica Patrick (who won her first career IndyCar race at the IndyCar Japan 300).

No matter who you are or what you do, you have lost. You have been on the losing end of promotions. You have been on the losing end of relationships. You have been on the losing end of sale pitches. You have lost at one time or another.

Moreover, when you have lost, it was no doubt a painful experience. As renowned author and speaker John C. Maxwell has remarked in several of his books, "When we are winning nothing hurts; when we are losing everything hurts."

The reality, however, is that life is not an endless progression of forward progress – accomplishment after accomplishment ... achievement after achievement ... victory after victory. Eventually you will endure a setback.

How do you feel when things are not going so well? You might tend to take on a miserable disposition. Your mind might magnify any little annoyance or trouble. You might even thrust your dismal state onto those around you. You certainly are stoic and less fun loving. You become distracted or preoccupied.

Nevertheless, there is nothing to say that you cannot fight to work through the effects of this discontentment and not allow it to affect those around you. Put the setback or disappointment in perspective. Just how vital is it compared to your entire life, business, or career? The chances are from an overall perspective the setback is likely relatively small.

Additionally, remind yourself that the setback does not define you. It does not undo your prior accomplishments and achievements. Thus, you still have an entire body of work to be proud of.

Also remember that loss is not fatal. Even those behind the greatest accomplishments throughout history suffered previous setbacks equivalent to losses. So what? Pick yourself up and continue to pursue your goals.

Finally, with every setback or disappointment, you have gained something. It may be experience. It may be better relationships with those around you. It may be a better understanding of those who support you. You need to take inventory of what you gained from your setbacks and truly appreciate it. This may be the best outcome to get you to your goals.

Chapter 32
Winning By Taking Second

Do The Right Thing, No Matter The Cost. You Win In The End.

On December 22, 2012, Spain's Iván Frenández Anaya was competing in a cross-country race in Burlada, a municipality in northern Spain. Those in his home country considered him an up and coming talent for the country with respect to distance running. In fact, two years earlier he was the national champion at the 5,000-meter distance.

On this particular day in this race, however, Anaya was firmly in second place. With 150 meters to go, he was behind by about 20 meters, a considerable lead to overcome with such a short distance to go. While he resolved himself to a second place finish, he pressed forward.

While Anaya was significantly behind the lead runner much of the race, as he made the turn towards the short run up to the finish line he felt that he was rapidly gaining ground on top place. Anaya dug into his energy reserves, lengthened his stride, and willed himself forward. He was a consummate competitor. As such his drive was almost instinctive.

He was about to overtake the lead runner, a Kenyan named Abel Mutai. At the last moment, however, Anaya geared down explicably. He maneuvered behind the lead runner.

Mutai, an Olympic bronze medalist in the 3,000-meter steeplechase, had led the entire race. Short of the finish line, however, he mistakenly thought he had completed the course. In so thinking, he reduced his gait to a mere walk.

Spectators seeing Mutai's mistake shouted at him, encouraging him to go the final few meters to victory. He did not understand. Their comments were meaningless. He did not speak Spanish.

As competitive as Anaya was, his character trumped it. He could not take advantage of Mutai's misunderstanding. In a show of sportsmanship and class, he ushered the Kenyan across the finish line in first place, taking what he believed was his rightful place – second.

While Anaya did not win this particular cross-country race, he won something more important – the admiration of others.

Often in life (whether in business or your personal dealings), you will be faced with difficult dilemmas. While these dilemmas may not quite rise up to a decision between being honest or not, they still serve to challenge your integrity.

It might relate to taking responsibility for something that does not go as planned. It might relate to sharing the credit with others (or completely surrendering it to them). It might relate to taking advantage of someone's innocent blunder. Whatever the case, you will encounter these situations.

Yes, being honesty is vital and is non-negotiable in establishing any sort of integrity. While doing the right thing may not be as vital, understand that it is important if you want others to consider you as having great character.

Chapter 33
Find Your Greatness

Know That In Every Victory And In Every Defeat, You Have Achieved Something.

On a beautiful, sunny November afternoon in Columbus, Ohio, the St. Francis DeSales girls' soccer team stormed the field at Crew Stadium as the final second elapsed in the Ohio High School Athletic Association Division II state championship game. Admist screams, cheers and a few moist eyes, the players ran onto the soccer pitch to greet their onfield teammates.

The scene seemed to be nothing out of the ordinary, except for one thing: At the hands of high school soccer power Cuyahoga Falls Walsh Jesuit, the Stallion girls had just lost, suffering the worst championship game defeat in Ohio high school girls' soccer history – five to nothing.

There is nothing to celebrate on the heels of a sound drubbing, especially when it occurs before faithful family, hundreds of friends and two bus-loads of classmates. Nevertheless, while there was certainly disappointment (especially amongst the six unassuming seniors), the DeSales high school girls still found reason to share a celebratory moment together.

When the 2012 OHSAA Division II high school girls' soccer tournament began in mid-October, there were 176 teams eligible to win a State title. At that time, no one thought that the Stallion girls had much of a chance. Afterall, leading up to the single-elimination tournament, they had lost their last five games and their regular season record was far from spectacular.

Further, while they were projected to easily get beyond the first round, there were some who predicted that this injury-hampered team might lose in the second round against a strong area opponent.

The second round loss did not happen, however. Nor did it in the third round against their sturdy league rival.

Certainly, however, many felt they would lose in the District championship. After all, they were playing against the number one seed, a team that had easily bested them in the regular season. The Stallion women, however, grew deaf to the prognosticators, scoring in overtime to ensure that the season would continue.

"Surely, they will not make it out of regional play," Stallion detractors thought. The odds were against them. In the regional semi-final, they played a top seed from another district. Nevertheless, they won again, scoring in the final minute of regulation.

And after the remanants of Hurricane Sandy delayed the regional semi-final game for two days, the St. Francis DeSales girls' soccer team were forced to play the regional championship game less then 48 hours later. Despite squaring off against another highly-seeded team that had four days of rest, they managed to win again.

Then in the State semi-final, they embarked upon another "seemingly insurmountable challenge" as they faced a perennial soccer power from the Cincinnati area with a consensus All-American player. But once again, the Stallions found a way to score and turn away the final several minutes of desperate onslaught from their opponent.

When the state tournamement began, no one had any reason to suspect that the St. Francis DeSales Stallions would be in the title game. On November 9th, however, there they were, in their uniforms, on the field and ready to play.

Interestingly enough, before each game – almost as a ritual or tradition – each Stallion player wraps a single piece of athletic tape around their forearm. Then using a felt tipped marker they write on it, *Find Your Greatness*. These three simple words serve as a reminder that with every game, practice or soccer encounter, there is something to achieve beyond mere wins.

So perhaps it is not surprising that the DeSales girls ran onto the field in celebration after what others might deem a stunning defeat. They realized that while they might not have won, they had got to where 174 other teams failed to get.

And despite suffering a crushing defeat, all 22 girls played their hearts out until those final seconds ticked away. And despite not reaching the absolute pinnacle of Ohio high school soccer, they knew they had still achieved something. And that something was certainly enough to satisfy their three-word mantra and justify storming the field in celebration.

What is your greatness? Far too often, we hang our heads when things do not go exactly our way. Rather, we should follow the lead of the St. Francis DeSales girls' soccer team and take an inventory of all we have as opposed to all we don't.

While you might not achieve all your dreams or conquer every challenge, there is always something to celebrate. You are not going to close every sale, but you are close enough to celebrate. You might be seemingly overlooked for that promotion, but that does not erase all that you have achieved. You might not have a business that is featured in the *Wall Street Journal* (or even your local Main Street Journal), but you still offer great value to your community.

With every setback or disappointment, take some time to collect yourself. In those moments, reflect back on all you have done and ignore what you have not. In that quiet time to yourself, imagine the words "*Find Your Greatness*" and as you do, storm the field in your heart with celebration.

Chapter 34
The 3:59.4 Lesson

What Matters Most Is What You Believe To Be Your Abilities.

On May 6th, 1954, an unidentified announcer gave the results for the recently completed race in a track and field meet being held at Oxford University. As he uttered "In the one-mile run, with a first place winning time of three-minutes ...," the crowd interrupted him, cheering in sheer excitement.

The winner of the race, the new world record holder, and the first person to finish a mile in less than four minutes was Dr. Roger Bannister – a young medical student from Oxford University. His official time, once the crowd permitted the announcer to continue, was 3 minutes and 59.4 seconds.

In the years following Dr. Bannister's May 6, 1954 feat, hundreds of runners have run sub-four-minute miles (and some runners have achieved the feat hundreds of times themselves). In fact, later in May 1954, John Landy, a miler from Australia, also ran the mile in less than four minutes – lowering the world record for the mile to 3:58.0.

As of today, men over the age of 30 have run miles in less than four minutes as well as men over the age of 40. There are also women within striking distance of the sub-four-minute milestone. Currently, the world record is more than 15 seconds under four minutes.

Prior to Dr. Bannister's accomplishment, however, few believed that a human would ever break the four-minute-mile barrier. Experts from the athletic, medical, and scientific community regarded running a sub-four-minute mile as an insurmountable limitation of the human body. After all, the previous world record of 4:01.3 had stood unchanged for nine years.

Despite what the experts said, Bannister thought otherwise. In his mind, it was not a question of whether or not someone could run a sub-four-minute mile. For Bannister the questions to be answered were "who" and "when."

Bannister believed that someone would break the four-minute barrier. He believed that he was capable of doing it. He believed that his unique training methods would enable him to. And, in the end, his convictions and confidence carried him to world-renowned prominence.

The story of Dr. Roger Bannister's sub-four-minute mile has a simple lesson for us in life. That lesson is that what others believe to be your abilities and limitations has absolutely no bearing on how high you can take yourself. What does matter ultimately (and primarily), however, is *what you believe to be your abilities and limitations.*

Each of you needs to believe that within you is a "sub-four-minute" type performance regarding your achievement, whether in sales, the sciences, or just being a good parent. To be successful, you need to cast aside the thoughts of naysayers. You need to believe that you have that performance where you quash all self-doubt and assume a "not if, but when" confidence. You need to endeavor to amaze those around you who do not believe.

The lesson that Dr. Roger Bannister gave us in a particular 3 minutes, 59.4 seconds span of his life, is that for us to be as successful as we can be, the starting point is we simply need to *believe.*

Chapter 35
Hanging On By A Finger

Life Will Throw Difficult Choices At You. Get Used To It.

It is not easy to describe the passion with which many athletes approach their sports. For some, it is the only thing keeping them in school or motivating them to go to college. For others, it is an escape from a less than ideal situation. For many, it is just an indescribable feeling – a sense of belonging, a feeling of accomplishment, or thrill of a challenge that they simply cannot duplicate anywhere else.

Whatever the case, many athletes pour themselves into their sport or sports. They arrive at practice early and stay late, manage their entire day in contemplation of the competing game, and use every possible spare conscious moment to think on their athletic craft.

In their mind, the preseason starts the moment the last season ends. From that point, they make every day count – developing physical stamina, agility, and muscle memory. It is all in the name of getting better and being their best.

This cycle continues. It continues for as long as it possibly can. For some, days of competing ends sometime before they are out of high school. For others, they get to participate in their sport at the collegiate level. For a very fortunate few, they earn a living playing the sport they love. For everyone, however, eventually that final game, inning, or race comes.

Although that day eventually comes for all athletes, while they compete they will sacrifice much to keep playing. Ask Trevor Wikre.

With an enrollment of around 9,000 students, Mesa State University is a comprehensive public institute of higher education in Grand Junction, Colorado. While Mavericks football is on few people's "must watch" list in the fall and while no one considers it a feeder for the National Football League, it is a respectable NCAA Division

II football program. The young men that choose to play there love the sport, are committed to playing it at a high level, and have done so for years.

Trevor fit this profile. He had been playing football since he was seven. In the fall of 2008, he was 21 and had built himself through training to a sturdy 6'3", 280-pound football player. After years of paying his dues, he earned the distinction of being a starting offensive guard for what was his senior (and, likely, final) season.

On September 30, however, something happened to Trevor that had never happened to him before. He was injured. During practice, somehow, he caught his finger in a teammate's jersey. There was a tug, a twist, and then an "odd" sensation.

When he took off his glove, it became clear. He had suffered a compound fracture to his right pinkie finger. In short, the finger was not only broken but the bone was protruding through the skin.

Doctors gave him the worse possible news: It was a season-ending injury. In fact, the break was so horrific that they would have to use pins to keep the bone in place while it healed. Even then, there was no guarantee that the finger would heal straight.

Faced with this predicament, Trevor made a hard decision. It was a decision that few of us would consider. It was a decision with which the doctor was not completely comfortable. Nevertheless, Trevor made it.

Trevor instructed the doctor to amputate the injured finger below the second joint. Sure, the loss of his pinkie created inconveniences that a person with ten digits could not comprehend. In addition, it likely creates the occasional double take from onlookers. Moreover, he will certainly have to continually be hit with the question, "What happened?"

What this decision did, however, was allow him to continue to do what he loves – play football. As Trevor said in his interview with *People* magazine, "It would have been harder to say goodbye to my last year of football than to my finger. It was my senior year. I didn't want to sit it out."

While it might not come down to losing appendages, life will throw difficult choices at you. You might have to choose between staying close to family or foregoing a wonderful career opportunity. You might have to choose between that dream house or caring for an ailing relative. You might have to choose between terminating an employee or sacrificing the Disney vacation you have promised your family.

Life will throw difficult choices at you. It is up to you to determine what is really important to you and make a decision no matter how hard it might be.

Chapter 36
A Perfect Mistake

Always Be Open To Contrition And Forgiveness.

Over 130+ years of Major League Baseball (MLB), there have been roughly 300,000 baseball games played. Of all those games, less than a couple dozen have been considered "perfect." That works out to one perfect game every 13,000 to 14,000 games, or one every five or six years.

A perfect game is defined by MLB as a game in which a pitcher pitches a victory that lasts a minimum of nine innings and in which no opposing player reaches base. Thus, the pitcher cannot allow any hits, walks, hit batsmen, or any opposing player to reach base safely for any other reason. In the simplest of terms, the pitcher can only pitch to 27 batters.

Perfection is something we normally do not expect from sports. In football, coaches will tell you that there is a mistake on every play. In basketball, we don't expect anyone to make every shot they take, even from those who rely on lay-ups for scoring. Imperfection is simply part of sports. Everyone makes a mistake now and then.

So the notion that a pitcher can get through an entire game with no one on the opposing team getting on base is a remarkable feat. It, however, is more than a remarkable feat for the pitcher. As a pitcher moves closer to "perfection," the team rallies (albeit quietly) around the pending accomplishment. It goes beyond just the team, too. An entire fan base (whether near or far) will sit in anxious anticipation. In fact, as a pitcher approaches the "perfect game" milestone, almost anyone interested in sports has a heightened interest in the situation.

That was exactly the mood at Comeria Park in Detroit, Michigan on June 2nd, 2010, as Detroit Tiger pitcher Armando Galarraga was preparing to pitch with two outs in the top of the ninth inning. The Detroit Tigers were hosting the Cleveland Indians in what was supposed to be just another game. As the game wore on, however, it became clear that this was not just any old American League Central Division contest.

Offensively, the game had no real significance. Detroit scored a run on a second-inning solo home run. The Tigers then scored two more runs in the eighth on a sequence of base hits and a Cleveland throwing error. It was Detroit's pitcher, however, that created the excitement.

Galarraga was the starting pitcher for the Tigers. In the first inning, the Indians sent three batters to the plate. In succession, the Tigers' pitcher sent them back to the dugout with an out. This happened again in the second as well as the third. In fact, this scenario played out for another five innings.

After eight innings, Galarraga had faced 24 batters and each failed to reach first base. There was a tension building throughout the ballpark. The Detroit pitcher was three outs away from a perfect game, something that had never happened in the Tiger's 110-year history.

Adding to the tension was the manner in which Galarraga had got to this point. While his pitching was spectacular, this had been a team effort. Of the 24 batters who returned to the Indian dugout with nothing to show for their effort, 11 were the result of an incredible effort by Tiger infielders and outfielders.

This team effort continued in the ninth inning. Tiger Austin Jackson saved the perfect game, making an over-the-shoulder catch to retire the 25th batter. Then the Tiger infield successfully fielded a routine ground ball and made a timely throw to first base to dispatch the 26th batter.

Immediately fans took to their feet and began applauding encouragement towards Galarraga. To this point, he had faced 26 batters and recorded 26 outs. He was on the precipice of perfection, as a unique air of anxiety and excitement filled the ballpark.

Galarraga fired the first pitch. It was a called strike, right down the middle. The cheering heightened. He was moving closer still to the perfect game.

The second pitch slapped the catcher's glove. "Ball," the umpire motioned. The partisan crowd bemoaned the call. Nevertheless, they quickly shook off the disappointment, and then began cheering in earnest.

With a one-and-one count, Galarraga wound up to pitch as he had done thousands of times before and 82 times that day. He made a smooth motion, and then fired the ball towards the plate. The crowd held its collective breath for the split second it took the ball to travel from the mound to the plate.

"Crack!" The Indian's batter connected with the ball.

The connection, however, was hardly substantial. The ball came off the bat, hit the ground a few yards in front of the batter, and began to lose momentum as it rolled between first and second base.

It was a routine ground ball. One that the Detroit Tigers had executed hundreds of times that season alone in practice, warm-ups and games. The first baseman moved into position to field the gently rolling ball. The second baseman maneuvered a few yards behind him, just in case. And Armando Galarraga dashed over to cover first base, in anticipation of the throw.

Just as they had planned and practiced, the defensive play materialized. The ball flew off the bat to the first baseman. He then perfectly fielded the ball and methodically threw it towards first base.

There Armando Galarraga was waiting. His glove was outstretched, ready to receive the ball. At the same time, he was mindful to have a foot firmly on the base, as he knew that the Cleveland Indian batter was desperately trying to beat the throw.

Bing. Bang. Boom. The throw was on target and in time. The team tallied the final out. Galarraga achieved perfection.

The Tiger fans cheered wildly. Galarraga jumped up in elation. The Detroit players immediately began moving towards him, looking to join in.

A split second after the celebration started, however, it ended. At first, there was some confusion as to why. Then it became clear. First base umpire Jim Joyce held his arms out to his side, horizontal to the ground.

"Safe," is what Joyce indicated, effectively ruling that the base runner had in fact beaten the throw to first. Just like that, the perfect game was lost.

Galarraga and other Tiger players looked in disbelief at umpire Joyce. Fans screamed a chorus of expletives from the stands. Announcers were at a loss for words.

In this electronic age, however, the replay of the previous play was immediate. On close circuit monitors for announcers. On the stadium screens for Comerica Park fans. On televisions and the Internet across the country. For everyone to see, Jim Joyce's call was wrong.

In fact, it was not even close. Armando Galarraga clearly had the ball in his glove and foot on first base almost a full half-second before the runner arrived. There was no question. Joyce should have called the batter out.

As for the game, other than Tiger Manager Jim Leyland quietly confronting Joyce, there was no official protest. The game simply continued, like any other game. The Cleveland Indians sent their 28th person to the batter box, the Tigers recorded another out, and the game ended 3-0.

Outside the game, however, there was an immediate firestorm of controversy. While most acknowledged that the errant call deprived Armando Galarraga of a well deserved achievement, deep down inside everyone felt a sense of being cheated too.

The entire sports media felt robbed of being able to cover a perfect game. They openly questioned, "How could Jim Joyce made such an obvious error at such an inappropriate time?"

Fans at the game, fans of the Detroit Tigers, and even fans of baseball had been witnesses to the rarest of baseball achievements – the perfect game. Almost in unison, they began an attack on the first base umpire. Using social media, talk radio, and open protest, they expressed genuine anger and hatred towards Jim Joyce's call. There were cries for answers. There were demands for Joyce's suspension. There were calls for his outright and immediate dismissal.

This was nowhere near the first questionable call in MLB history. The media and partisan fans question umpire decisions in almost every game. Strikes that should be balls; balls that should be strikes. Foul balls that should be fair; fair balls that should be foul. Runners who should be safe; runners who should be out.

By in large, umpires are deaf to the din of noise created by media and fans. They make their calls, however flawed they might be. Then they move on to the next game, perhaps in a different city, likely overseeing new teams with their own ravenous fans. In so doing, they completely shake off whatever mistakes they might have made. No explanation. No justification. No commentary. Nothing.

This mistake, however, was not likely to go away. There was genuine anger surrounding Jim Joyce's call. Moreover, that anger seemed to be bubbling up. And it was not going to die down until MLB provided the situation some degree of satisfaction – a call reversal ... a suspension ... something.

Just as the situation seemed to be heading towards a flashpoint, Jim Joyce stepped forward and addressed the situation. He did not defend his call. He made no excuses for the call. He made no justifications. He offered no reasoning.

Rather Joyce did something uncharacteristic for his profession. After seeing the replay for himself after the game, he admitted his mistake. He emotionally remarked, "It was the biggest call of my career and I kicked it. I just cost that kid a perfect game."

More than just owning his mistake, Joyce further broke from baseball tradition. He requested that the Detroit Tigers allow him a moment to speak with Armando Galarraga. With that opportunity, Joyce made a heartfelt apology to Galarraga.

While Joyce's admission and subsequent apology served to satisfy many, there were still smoldering embers of anger and resentment amongst baseball fans and media. Galarraga could have seized upon this and carried on as a victim. He could have played up the tragedy of the situation. He could have harbored resentment towards Joyce and MLB refusing to overrule the call. Any or all of these would almost be expected in this day and age.

Galarraga did none of this, however. Rather, he used the attention that the media and fan base gave him to defend Jim Joyce, offer support for his work as an umpire, and forgive him for his honest mistake. In so doing, Galarraga completely extinguished any controversy and anger surrounding the blown call.

While Armando Galarraga will not go down as having a perfect game on June 2nd, 2010, the situation surrounding that game provides a perfect illustration for us to follow. First, you are only human. You have a propensity toward imperfection. As such, you have no doubt made mistakes. And you will no doubt make more. This is part of life. If you make a mistake and it hurts another – even though you diligently work to minimize the effect – never be too proud to say, "I am sorry."

Just speaking these words might not right the wrong or repair the damage to another. Nevertheless, an apology is always the first step. If nothing else, this simple action serves to diminish (if not completely eliminate) any resentment your mistake might have created.

Alternatively, as your existence involves other humans, no doubt others have wronged you and likely will in the future – hopefully inadvertently, but some possibly intentionally. Whatever the situation (and whether or not the wrongdoer has apologized to you), find the courage to forgive.

Forgiveness is a powerful thing. It gives comfort to others who are looking to associate with you. More importantly, however, it is mentally cleansing for you, as if help you cease feeling anger or resentful.

Chapter 37
The "Around The World" Walk-On

It Is Never Too Late To Embark On Something New.

In October 2012, Brian Rice walked on to the basketball team at NCAA Division III Geneva College, in Beaver Falls, Pennsylvania. Like other freshman, Rice hoped to help the Golden Tornadoes compete for a Presidents' Athletic Conference title, playing before 3,000 rowdy fans in Metheny Fieldhouse, and generally be a part of carrying on the college's basketball tradition.

It was, however, a long walk onto the Geneva College basketball team. Certainly, the journey began on the basketball team at New Castle (Pennsylvania) High School. There he considered making a run at playing NCAA Division II basketball somewhere. After all, he was a 6-foot-2 shooting guard that averaged 15 points and six rebounds per game.

That, however, was just the beginning of Rice's long walk onto Coach Jeff Santarsiero's Golden Tornadoes team. In fact, the walk was not just long, but also rather circuitous.

Enlisting in the Navy immediately after high school, Rice traveled to over 60 different countries on six continents. He served on everything from carriers to special patrol boats that transported Navy SEALs.

When time permitted, he continued to hone his basketball skills on ships, in ports and on bases across the world. In fact, while based in Italy, he played on a team that traveled and competed across Europe.

During his stint in the Navy, he worked his way through the ranks, eventually becoming a chief petty officer, which is just two notches below the highest enlisted classification. Here he was in charge of as many as 30 to 40 enlisted personnel.

After over 24 years in the Navy, Rice retired from the military. At 43-years-old, he decided to pursue his Bachelor's Degree in religious studies and selected Geneva College. Despite being twice the age of most college players (and having his own children who are just as old), he networked through a basketball coach friend into a walk-on tryout for the college team.

It is possible that Rice found inspiration from Raymond Aaron. Living in Richmond Hill, Ontario, Aaron heads a coaching and consulting practice that teaches people greater wealth, branding, recognition, confidence, respect, and authority. He helps his clients by drawing on his own experiences as a teacher, entrepreneur, and author.

At age 62, he heard of the Polar Race. This is a three-week ordeal where a handful of extreme athletes travel 350 miles across arctic ice-fields to reach the Magnetic North Pole. The catch is that in this race participants propel themselves using only skis with no motors.

Intrigued, Aaron signed on and diligently prepared himself. In 2007, he not only started the Polar Race, but also finished amongst competitors half his age. In so doing, he spent April in the Arctic traveling the equivalent of a marathon a day pulling a 100-pound sled. As he did, he endured the hardships of subzero temperatures, the rapid loss of weight, and the risk of polar bears.

Whatever your history and whatever path your life has taken you, you are never too old to take on something new.

Chapter 38
The Slowest Runner In America

You Don't Have To Be The Best.
You Just Need To Try Your Best.

Ben Comen was a remarkable athlete at Anderson, South Carolina's L.T. Hanna High School. People did not know him for bone-crushing solo tackles, acrobatic one-handed end-zone catch, or anything related to football. People did not know him for dead-on three-point shooting, suffocating defense or anything basketball. Nor did people know him for his tireless effort on the soccer pitch, his prowess as a lacrosse attacker, or ruthless spikes over the volleyball net.

In 2003, Ben ran cross country. Nevertheless, he was a remarkable athlete for the Yellow Jackets. It was not for any course or school records. It was not for consecutive races run. It was not for any first place finishes. Ben was notable simply because he finished.

Dubbed by *Sports Illustrated's* Rick Reilly as the slowest runner in America, Ben Comen has cerebral palsy. The condition did not affect his cognitive skills. In the classroom, he kept pace academically with his twin brother, Alex. On the course, however, his brother had him soundly beat moments after the starter gun sounded.

Generally caused by complications at birth, cerebral palsy is a condition that affects motor skills. As a part of it, the spine can become misaligned, impacting posture. Muscle development is impaired. Motor reflexes slow. Movement and balance become abnormal. Muscles tighten. Joints stiffen inexplicably. Knees knock. Feet drag. Running strides are inconsistent. Coordination is unreliable.

As a result, while Ben's running peers compete with one another for positioning and placing, he fought with himself. He battled to stay upright – small rocks, sticks, or any minor undulation on the course would send him sprawling to the ground. He struggled with exhaustion – expending extraordinary energy to make whatever progress he could.

While lead runners were crossing the tape, Ben was only a little over a quarter of the way done. When most runners had finished, he still had another half the course to traverse.

At this point, anyone else might consider giving up – declaring defeat and stop running altogether. Ben did not.

No matter the reason he fell, Ben got up. No matter how hard he fell, he got up. No matter how far he was behind, he continued. No matter how dirty, scraped, and bruised, he would march on towards the finish. No matter the weather conditions – scorching heat or diving rain – he pressed on.

Certainly, there is a message herein about perseverance. That is almost too obvious, however. The lesson is bigger than just that. You see, Ben did not persevere in an attempt to demonstrate his tenacity – though, clearly, it was evident. He did not persevere to become the best – he made no pretenses about that. He did not even persevere to gain over anyone else – in fact, he took last in every race.

Ben Comen persevered simply to compete against himself. With each race, he persisted and endured, simply to be better than he was before. He scrapped and bruised his body to record a faster time than the one before. In short, he struggled and battled to do his best – ultimately in his final attempt to run a sub-41 minute race.

Every day, compete with yourself. Do not make any day about trying to be *the best*. Do not make any day about being better than someone else is. Rather make every day be about doing *your best*.

With whatever life has given you, make your daily struggle about being a better version of yourself compared to the day before. You should battle to be a better person. You should persevere to be a better employer, employee, parent, child, and friend. Greatness is not about being the best. It is about doing your best.

Chapter 39
A Rookie Back-Up

To Do The Things You Want, Sometimes You Have To Do The Things You Don't.

On January 12, 2013, the Fond du Lac Cardinals drove the four-plus hours due north to Hancock, Michigan to face off against the host high school hockey team – the Hancock Bulldogs. As they travelled, they were hopeful that an additional victory would strengthen their position as the number two high school hockey team in the state of Wisconsin. After all, they were playing a team from Michigan's Copper Country – essentially the northern civilized tip of Michigan's Upper Peninsula, which is known for great high school hockey across the entire Midwest.

The Cardinal coaches, players and fans were, after all, very optimistic of a victory. For starters, they had a great team and it was rolling – claiming 13 wins to no defeats in its 2012-13 season. Furthermore, while Hancock was traditionally a high school hockey power, this year's Bulldog team was down – to this point it had a record below .500.

The play of the visiting Fond du Lac lived up to expectation. Over three periods of heated high school hockey, the Cardinals had 43 shots on goal. Almost anyone knowing anything about hockey would deem that an incredible offensive showing.

What Wisconsin's No. 2 team did not count on, however, was that Hancock's goalie would play like a college All-American. Hancock's Jacob Givens turned away all 43 shots. While the junior net minder only saw average action in the first period, the Cardinals brought an incredible onslaught of shots in the second and third. Nevertheless, in those final two periods Givens came through with 18 and 17 saves, respectively.

Givens made routine saves. He also stopped blistering shots from various angles. He took in long shots, snared ones from point-blank range, and handled ones in between. He covered up rebounds and made heady decision after heady decision. And, he had to make more than his share of sprawling acrobatic saves, one within the final minute of play.

In the end, Givens earned a shoot out. In addition to that, however, his 43-save heroics coupled with a third-period goal by his teammate, Brett Lepisto, helped the Bulldogs claim victory over the number two team in the state of Wisconsin.

It was no doubt a long ride back towards Green Bay, Wisconsin for the visiting Fond du Lac Cardinals. After all, they now had a blemish on their record and it came at the hands of a team with a losing record. What was likely most troubling, however, was that the player who had the biggest hand in defeating them was nothing more than a rookie back-up.

One week earlier, Jacob Given was the back-up goalie for the Hancock Bulldogs. In fact, a year earlier, the junior goaltender was not even playing hockey at all.

Competition to play high school hockey in Michigan's Copper Country is fierce. Furthermore, as equipment and the cost of ice time make hockey an expensive sport, most high schools do not roster junior varsity or development teams. Thus, if a Hancock student does not make the high school hockey team, they have to play in a recreational program (the Copper Country Junior Hockey Association), move on to another sport, or just sit out all together.

As a freshman, though he really wanted to play for the Bulldogs, Givens did not make the high school hockey team. Freshmen seldom do. The size and experience of the upperclassman generally win out. Givens figured he would give it another shot the next season.

As a sophomore, as much as he prepared and wanted to, Givens again did not make the team. The Hancock Bulldogs had a full complement of defensemen, the position he played. Givens chose to sit out, perhaps surmising that just maybe his dream to play high school hockey was not meant to be.

As tryouts for the Hancock High School hockey team drew closer in the fall of 2012, Givens once again felt that yearning to play high school hockey for his beloved Bulldogs. He, however, knew that the team still had a solid stable of defensemen returning.

Nevertheless, he really wanted to make the team. He wanted to be able to tell people that he was part of the Hancock Bulldog hockey team. He wanted to be part of the fanfare – announced at pep assemblies and receive accolades of classmates in the hallways. Moreover, he wanted to wear his game jerseys to school on the day of the game. He really wanted to be part of the team.

He knew, however, that Coach Dan Rouleau only had one goalie. Furthermore, Givens had some experience at that position in his younger years. Playing goalie was not necessarily the position that he wanted to play. Givens knew, however, that if he was willing to be the back-up goalie for Hancock High School, he could get what he truly wanted – to be on the Hancock Bulldog hockey team.

Life is full of things we don't want to do. We all want to start at the top and no one likes doing certain things, whether on a team or in the office. The reality is, however, that if you are willing to do the things that you don't want to do, in time you will get to do the things that you do.

Chapter 40
What's In A Name

There Is Great Value In Knowing The Names Of Others.

In 1989, the late Bo Schembechler, the legendary football coach of the University of Michigan, released his book *Bo*. Near the end, he relates what he describes as "the most significant lesson I ever learned in football." It did not involve a game against Ohio State or any trip to the Rose Bowl. It involved his son, Chip.

When Chip was in high school, he was on the football team. Although he loved the sport and was happy to be on the team, Schembechler's son was merely a back-up. In fact, according to the Michigan coach, Chip was one of the last guys to make the team.

One day during the season, Chip received a telephone call from the coach. Apparently, another player on the team would be returning punts in the next game. As this player's game pants did not fit, the coach told this player that he could have Chip's. The coach informed Chip of this and told him he would just have to wear his practice pants for the game. Understandably this upset Schembechler's son.

From there, Schembechler transitioned into a discussion about the players at Michigan. Like any other major college football program, Michigan has in excess 100 players each year. Although some of these players Schembechler concludes he "wouldn't put in a high school game" and others would be deemed as "awful," he considers every one of them part of the team. As such, Schembechler ensured that while he was coaching at Michigan that all players, whether a walk-on or a player destined for stardom in the NFL, were dressed in full uniform.

In addition, the Michigan coach made sure that each and every Wolverine player had his name sewn across the back of his jersey. This was extremely important. Why? This was because Schembechler knew that somewhere up in the stands, there was a mother and father watching. And whether their son was great, good or down right pitiful, they took pride in them. Ensuring that each players' name was properly displayed honored that.

No doubt, your name is important to you. You appreciate having it spelled correctly (or at least don't appreciate it when it's not). Moreover, you prefer to have it spelled correctly. Thus, if it is important to you, then someone else's name is just as important to them. Knowing this, it is one of the best compliments you can bestow upon someone – remembering their name (as well as spelling and pronouncing it correctly).

What is in a name? Whether you are an Ohio State Buckeye, a Michigan State Spartan or a Notre Dame Fighting Irish, you would have to agree with Coach Schembechler. What is in a name is everything – caring, honor, and respect.

Chapter 41
The Drought

Whatever The Circumstance, Keep After It. Eventually, You Will Break Through.

On February 22, 2011, almost 390 fans stood quietly in California Institute of Technology's Braun Gym. There was noticeable tension in the air. With just 3.3 seconds left in the game, the game was tied. To this point, host Caltech Beavers and the visiting, conference rival Occidental College Tigers each had 45 points.

Caltech, however, had the advantage. Their starting guard, Ryan Elmquist, was preparing to take two free throws. As one of the all-time leading scorers in Caltech basketball history, the home fans were hopeful that Elmquist could make at least one free throw.

 Certainly, this was a position that most every basketball player dreams of. The game is down to the final few seconds, the score is tied, and you are at the line with a chance to win it. This moment, however, was even more significant for the Caltech faithful. The men's basketball program was in the midst of a notable conference-losing streak.

Caltech was a member of the Southern California Intercollegiate Athletic Conference (SCIAC). Along with Occidental College (and three other Southern California institutions), they helped form the SCIAC in 1915. Other than a brief four-year hiatus from the Conference, Caltech had been a consistent part of the organization it helped form to promote and govern "competition in intercollegiate sports with the fundamental principle of the conference being to encourage the highest ideals of amateur sports in an environment of high academic standards."

Despite being a solid member of the SCIAC for almost 100 years, heading into this final game they had not won a game in Conference play all season. In fact, they had not won a SCIAC game in the prior season either. For that matter, it had not won a Conference game the season before that either. Or the season before that. Or before that.

On January 23, 1985, Caltech edged the Leopards from the University of La Verne 48-47. Since that game – a span of over 26 years – the Beavers had not been able to best a SCIAC foe in men's basketball. Caltech had come close on many occasions. Nevertheless, when Ryan Elmquist was preparing to shoot his free throws, the small private college in Pasadena, California was in the midst of a winning drought that spanned 310 games (and was longer than Elmquist or any current Caltech player was alive).

During this drought, however, Caltech never gave up. The college continued to field a men's basketball program. It continued to search for the right coach. It continued investing in facilities.

During this drought, the staff never gave up. The Caltech student recruiters sought the best basketball players, even though it had to work within academic standards that would rival any Ivy League school. The coaches (and there were only four in that period) worked the players just as hard as other conference opponents and other NCAA Division III programs.

During this drought, the players never gave up. Over the years, over 200 of them came, tried and gave it everything in each game. They worked hard in practice. They worked to develop themselves and their skills in the offseason.

When Ryan Elmquist knocked down his first free throw the 390 fans erupted, the basket was for more than just himself. It was for a dozen other teammates and a coach.

When the coach strategically directed Elmquist to miss his second free throw attempt to whittle away at the remaining game time, he did it for more than just the team. He did it for an entire student body, who were no doubt the brunt of jokes from friends who attended the SCIAC conference rivals.

When Braun Gymnasium erupted as the Occidental College 75-foot desperation heaved missed its mark and the final buzzer sounded, it was about more than the joy they felt in that moment. It was about an entire base of alumni and 25 teams that tried but could not get it done.

Everyone goes through droughts. Joblessness. A seemingly dying career. Professional setback after professional setback.

Everyone experiences that slump. Flat lined sales. Zero growth. Sagging profits.

Everyone experiences a famine of sorts for something. Ongoing relationship discord. Continual financial hardship. Health issue after health issue.

Whatever unpleasant circumstances you find yourself in, press on. As long as you keep after it, eventually that drought will end.

Chapter 42
We Are One

In The Grand Scheme Of Life, We Should Stand Together.

Sports and athletic competition are rife with rivalries, especially in college and high school football where generally these traditional adversaries do battle only once each year. Some of these great rivalries include Michigan-Ohio State (or Michigan State, depending on whom you ask) ... Notre Dame-USC ... Alabama-Auburn ... Florida-Georgia.

There are lesser known rivalries as well, such as. Capital U-Otterbein ... Beloit College-Lawrence University ... St. Olaf University-Carleton College ... Central Catholic Irish-St. Francis Knights ... DeSales Stallions-Watterson Eagles ... Hopkinton Hillers-Ashland Clockers ... Houghton Gremlins-Hancock Bulldogs. This list could go on and on.

Arguably, the most intense rivalry in football is the Army-Navy game. The intensity is in part due to the rivalry's longevity. With few interruptions, the annual epic battle between these two service academies goes back to 1890, when Navy beat Army at West Point, 24-0 and then Army exacted revenge the following year, dropping Navy 32-16 at Annapolis.

Further intensifying this rivalry is that over the year, the games' outcome has always seemed to have great significance. Before the lure of lucrative careers in the NFL and average collegiate players' size started to outpace the height and weight limitations at the service academies, the Army-Navy game often had national championship implications. Nevertheless, to this day the Commander-in-Chief's Trophy (awarded to each season's winner of the triangular series between Army, Navy, and Air Force) can hang in the balance on the outcome of this rivalry.

Driving this rivalry's intensity more than anything, however, is nothing more than bragging rights. Army and Navy do battle as the last football game of the season, Arch enemy versus arch enemy. Each side has only one chance to establish its superiority. Like mighty warriors, their respective institutions send them forth to defend the honor of their flag.

You can pay no heed to history. You can disregard their respective season record. You can ignore any statistic, fact, or figure. Each year the Army and Navy teams return, with hope upon hope, that they could overcome each other through a positive mental attitude, a little luck, and the sheer will to win.

This rivalry is bigger than football, however. Every Cadet at West Point lives and breathes the phrase "Beat Navy." At the same time, every Navy Midshipmen counter with, "Beat Army" (even the weight plates in Navy's Annapolis workout facilities are stamped with that mantra).

The importance of this rivalry's outcome, however, extends well beyond those enrolled at West Point and Annapolis. Anyone worldwide associated with the United States Army or Navy has an interest in this game.

This includes the Army's rank-and-file privates and on up through lieutenants, majors, and even generals. It also includes the Navy's lowest level ensigns and on up through petty officers, captains, as well as fleet commanders and admirals. This encompasses those serving in active duty as well as those who are now retired or somehow discharged from service. Even civilians with no prior service but just a particular affinity towards one or the other of these branches of military take up sides.

There are so many people with a rooting interest in this rivalry that other than the first few games, neither Army nor Navy has capacity in its respective home stadiums to accommodate the fandom. While as of late the Army-Navy game seems to have found sites approximately equidistant from each institution, over the year rivalry has been shared with various parts of America, including Yankee Stadium, the Rose Bowl, as well as Chicago's Soldier Field.

While the venue has changed, what they have been playing for has not. Pride. While the game is only football, a victory radiates pride on a seemingly much broader scale. It is as if victory for one's respective team somehow definitively signifies the overall superiority of that particular military branch.

This is what keeps the games fiercely competitive. This is what keeps the rivalry intense. This is what serves to keep this rivalry tradition alive.

While the tradition surrounding the game is alive, it is only part of the tradition involved with the Army-Navy game. Another traditional aspect of this rivalry follows the game and is of great importance to football players as well as Cadets and Midshipmen.

Despite the record of Army or Navy entering the game, Army and Navy uphold this tradition. Whether or not a national championship is on the line, they uphold this tradition. No matter who wins, no matter the score, and no matter what hard feelings may have developed during the game, players uphold this tradition.

At the end of the Army-Navy game, the winning team stands with the losing team facing the defeated fans (whether Cadets or Midshipmen), and respectfully joins in with the playing and singing of the losing team's school song. Then the losing team accompanies the winning team over to its side of the field, faces the victorious students, and returns the reverence.

While the Cadets and Midshipmen uphold this tradition as a show of mutual respect, they also do this as an indication of solidarity. Win or lose, the football Cadets share in a rendition of *Anchors Aweigh* and, in turn, win or lose the football Midshipmen will do the same for *On Brave Old Army Team*, as if to say, "We Are One."

Together, they signify, *We* are one military. Together, *We* stand as one nation. Together, *We* are one in defense of freedom and the American ideals of democracy. *We* are one and we will fight together. *We* are one and are willing to pay the ultimate sacrifice together or for each other. We Are One.

Life seems to be chocked full of rivalries. Political rivals. Corporate rivals. Religious rivals. Rivals for business, and rivals for attention, dollars, and affections.

In the grand scheme of human life, however, *We Are One*. While there are many rivalries in life, on a certain level we should stand together. At some point, we are more than just Michigan Wolverines, Ohio State Buckeyes, Florida Gators, or any other collegiate (or professional) team. At some point, Republicans, Democrats, and all political views unite in common cause (even if the approach differs).

At some point, we are not Europeans, Asians, or Americans. At some point, we cannot divvy up the human race into teams of Christianity, Judaism, Islam, or any other world religion.

We Are One. We are all human and we may be the only one of our kind. At some point, we need to stand together on this relatively tiny, water-covered rock the perfect distance from an appropriate star. We need to stand together against hunger, disease, and natural disasters of every kind.

We are one and we need to coordinate our knowledge and technology so that we ensure the survival of this species. We need to do this so that one day, our children's, children's, children can continue to proclaim, *We Are One*.

Chapter 43
Greatness Continues

Look Around You. Greatness Is There To Find.

Is this it? Does this book contain every obscure sporting event story? Do these pages encompass the complete list of young athletes demonstrating that perseverance pays off? Are these the only instances of sports competitors exhibiting acts of great compassion, sportsmanship, or determination? Hardly.

As I started working on this, the final chapter, I got distracted (as I often do when writing) by a week or two old copy of *The Columbus Dispatch*. There on the second page of the sports section was a story about Charlotte Brown.

Amidst stories about the Major League Baseball season, the National Basketball Association playoffs, and the local Ohio State Buckeyes was a story about this high school girl in Texas who was competing in the track and field Class 3A state championship. Charlotte Brown (Emory Rains High School) was one of the top qualifiers in the pole vault at 11 feet, 6 inches.

Although Brown only managed to clear 10 feet, 6 inches (well short of her personal best), she will likely be back as she is only a freshman. Though she only finished eighth out of the nine state qualifiers (and thus missing a medal), she left the track to a standing ovation from the several hundred people watching her event. Why? Brown is legally blind.

Charlotte Brown is legally blind. Yet she races down the pole vault runaway and somehow at the precise moment was able to plant the end of the 16-foot pole in an in-ground box that is less than two-feet across. From this point, she was able to launch herself 10-plus feet in the air over a crossbar that she cannot even see. If she can do this, what is holding you back from your goals and aspirations?

Inspiring? Absolutely. My point, however, is that the stories in this book are far from being comprehensive. This book only has stories that were within my radar. That is, some of these chapters are events I was fortunate enough to have witnessed firsthand. Others are ones I happened across reading newspapers from areas where I have a connection – more specifically, central Ohio, Beloit, Wisconsin, and Michigan's Copper Country. The balance, family, friends, and acquaintances shared with me (in fact, often when I mention this book project, the person I told would share with me something about a notable athlete, event, or circumstance that I was not aware).

There is, however, nothing special about my life, my network, or me. That is, I have no doubts that within the lives of others (or even your own) are athletes who are doing inspiring things. They are being courageous. They are being generous. They are doing many things that will leave you in awe.

Therefore, if you are looking for inspiration beyond what I have included in this book, I encourage you to go out and find it. You do not necessarily need to drop a few hundred dollars for parking, tickets, and overpriced refreshments at a professional game. For next to nothing, you can find these moment at almost any small college, high school, or recreational game.

Wherever you happen to stumble across that moment does not matter. What does, however, is that you take it in. Use that little act of greatness to somehow inspire you and propel you forward to wherever you are headed.

Once you have, however, please share that moment with me. I would greatly appreciate it – simply e-mail me at frankagin@amspirit.com.

About The Author

Frank J. Agin

Frank Agin is the founder and president of AmSpirit Business Connections, an organization that empowers entrepreneurs, sales representatives and professionals to become more successful through networking.

As AmSpirit Business Connections has grown, Frank has established himself as an authority on professional networking and business relationship development. He has written various articles on professional networking, is a sought after presenter on this topic (including using social media in business) and consults with companies and organizations on how to make a more effective use of business relationships.

Finally, Frank's the author and co-author of several books, listed on the pages that follow or at http://www.frankagin.com/

Along with having a CPA designation, he has an undergraduate economics and management degree from Beloit College (Beloit, Wisconsin) and an MBA and law degree from the Ohio State University. Contact him via e-mail (frankagin@amspirit.com)

LinkedWorking:

Generating Success on the World's Largest Professional Networking Website

"Success on LinkedIn follows all the same rules of traditional networking."

LinkedWorking is a professional development book aimed at helping individuals achieve great success on LinkedIn, the world's largest professional networking website. Released March 2009.

Foundational Networking:

Building Know, Like and Trust To Create A Lifetime of Extraordinary Success

"Become the person you want to network with"

Foundational Networking is a personal development book aimed at helping become better networkers by simply having better attitudes and habits. Released October 2008.

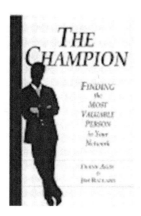

The Champion:

Finding the Most Valuable Person in Your Network

"Who Is The Most Valuable Person In Your Network?"

Are you looking for a Champion? Don't you sometimes wonder: "There must be someone out there who will set me up with all sorts of great ideas, wonderful opportunities, and incredible new contacts, so as to bring me the success I deserve." If this is your dream you've come to the right place. Destiny has brought you just a click away from the book that will help you find such an individual- The Champion. Released March 2010.

The Giving Journal:

Achieving Success Through Focused Generosity

"How Can You Give More To Others?"

Box Score & Statistics

The material, information, and facts and figures in Chase Greatness comes from various contacts and sources, as detailed below.

Chapter 2: The Game Of Change

Loyola tops Mississippi State in 'Game of Change' rematch, Toni Ginnetti, *Chicago Sun Times*, December 15, 2012

Game of Change' echoes through history, Fred Mitchell, *Chicago Tribune*, December 14, 2012

http://en.wikipedia.org/wiki/1963_NCAA_Men's_Division_I_Basketball_Tournament

Chapter 3: The Arsenal

This story I originally wrote for my book *Foundational Networking: Building Know, Like and Trust To Create A Lifetime Of Extraordinary Success.*

Chapter 4: Team Chemistry

Tacit knowledge as a source of competitive advantage in the National Basketball Association, Berman, S. L., J. Down and C. W. L. Hill, 2002, *The Academy of Management Journal* 45(1): 13-31.

Chapter 5: A Lesson From The Heartland

Wrestlers Share Magical Moment, Craig Sesker, *Omaha World-Herald*, December 17, 2003

Chapter 6: Six Kicks In The Summer

Tragedy to triumph: The amazing story of the Ishpeming Hematites, Jon Weirtheim, Viewpoint, SI.com. December 12, 2012.

Chapter 7: Great Scott!

9 Year Old Is "Too Good" to Play Baseball, Associated Press, 2008

"Too Good" to Play Baseball? Game Over, Kathy McManus, October 2, 2008

Chapter 8: The Octuple Co-Championship

8 overtimes, 2 champions: St. Mary's, Marquette are co-champs after 1-1 tie, Chris Lau, *Detroit Free Press* Sports Writer, , March 9, 2008.

Chapter 9: A Pitchless Win

Embree earns 'W' without throwing pitch, Thomas Harding (with contributions from Cheng Sio), MLB.com, July 8, 2009

Nationals' bloopers hand Embree win without a pitch, Troy E.Renek, *The Denver Post*, July 8, 2009

http://www.baseball-almanac.com/players/player.php?p=embrea01

Chapter 10: Life Is A Decathlon

The Decathlon: A colorful history of track and field's most challenging event, Frank Zarnowski. Pg. 188-191

Yang Chuan-kwang Obituary, UCLABruins.com (The Official Website Of UCLA Athletics), January 28, 2007

Chapter 11: An Awesome Kick

Interview with Casey Claxon, Head Girls Soccer Coach, Ridgewood High School (West Lafayette, Ohio), May 2013

RHS looks for big win, Jason West, *Coshocton Tribune*, October 26, 2012

Generals end season with win, Jason West, *Coshocton Tribune*, October 27, 2012

Chapter 12: Fourth & 15 Years

Beloit Daily News, November 8, 1982

Chapter 13: McNasty

McEnroe was McNasty on and off the court, Larry Schwartz, Sports Century Biography, ESPN.com, http://espn.go.com/classic/biography/s/McEnroe_John.html

Chapter 14: Still The Best Policy

This is an excerpt from *Foundational Networking: Building Know, Like And Trust To Create A Lifetime Of Extraordinary Success.*

Chapter 15: Do You Believe In Miracles?

The Boys of Winter: The Untold Story of a Coach, a Dream, and the 1980 U.S. Olympic Hockey Team, Wayne Coffey and Jim Craig, Crown Publishing Group, 2005

Chapter 16: Unstoppable

A Champ In, And Out Of, The Ring, Steve Hartman, CBS News, February 11, 2009

A fighting spirit, John Erardi, Enquirer, February 15, 2006, retrieved from:

www.bizzyblog.com/2006/02/15/positivity-if-you-think-hes-different-you-dont-know-dustin/

After two gruelling weeks, Phil Packer finishes a distant last but becomes a marathon *winner,* Julie Henry, The Sydney Morning Herald, May 11, 2009, retrieved from: smh.com.au

Disabled Vet – Told He Would Never Walk Again, Finishes Marathon For Charity,

freedomrebel, The Zoo, May 11, 2005, retrieved from: tpzoo.wordpress.com/2009/05/11/disabled-vet-told-he-would-never-walk-again-finishes-marathon-for-charity/

Finishing London Marathon... 2 Weeks Later, Mark Remy, Runner's World, May 8,

2009, retrieved from: http://m.runnersworld.com/finishing-london-marathon-2-weeks-later

High School Wrestler Dustin Carter's Simple Philosophy: 'I Wrestle Like Anybody Else',

Michael David Smith, AolNews. February 29, 2008

Injured soldier finishes London Marathon two weeks after starting, AFP, AFP Global

Edition, May 9, 2009, retrieved from: www.thefreelibrary.com/Injured+soldier+finishes+London+Marathon+two+weeks+after+starting-a01611865255

Man who wouldn't walk again finishes marathon, Richard Greene, CNN.com, May 13, 2009

Chapter 17: In The Face Of Tradition

Interview with Mary Lombardo Graves (mother of Jessica Stubitsch)

Interview with Kelly Van Lanen (mother of Morgan Van Lanen)

Erin Dimeglio ready to try her hand as South Plantation QB, The Miami Herald, Manny Navarro, August 8, 2012

Chapter 18: Four Eighteen

Interview With Lewis Howes

Faces In The Crowd, Sports Illustrated, November 4, 2002

Upper Midwest Athletic Conference starts next year, Chicago Tribune, September 15, 2002

http://www.umacathletics.com/custompages/statistics/fb/2002/MARTPRIN.HTM#GAME.PLY

http://cfreference.net/cfr/all-time-head-to-head/martin-luther-college/1926/vs/principia-college/1908

http://www.phys.utk.edu/sorensen/cfr/cfr/Output/2002/CF_2002_Team_Principia_College.html

Chapter 19: The Wizard Of Westwood

The Official Website of John Wooden (http://www.coachwooden.com)

Chapter 20: Shoeless Ron Hunter

Barefoot IUPUI coach helps collect 100,000 pairs of shoes, Associated Press, USA Today, January 25, 2008

Hunter coaches barefoot, and sneakers come flooding in, ESPN.com news services, ESPN.com, January 25, 2008

IUPUI coach goes barefoot again, and this time he's not alone, Eamonn Brennan, rivals.com, January 2008

Ron Hunter Coaches Barefoot for Charity, Matt Snyder, AOLNews.com, January 20, 2009

Chapter 21: Stand Tall!

To No Earthly King, Dr. Bill Mallon, M.D. and Ian Buchanan, *Journal Of Olympic History,* September 1999, pg 21-8

Chapter 22: Eleven Seconds To Courage

Eleven Seconds: A Story of Tragedy, Courage & Triumph, Travis Roy and E.M. Swift, Warner Books

This story is an excerpt from Frank Agin's book, *Foundational Networking: Building Know, Like And Trust To Create A Lifetime Of Extraordinary Success.*

Chapter 23: Standing O-H ... I-O

Tradition, Bo Schembechler with Dan Ewald, pg. 86-88

Chapter 24: Singles Score Runs Too!

Major League Baseball

This is an excerpt from my book, *Foundational Networking: Building Know, Like & Trust For A Lifetime Of Extraordinary Success.*

Chapter 25: Bonnie Richardson High

Small-town Texas track star Bonnie Richardson repeats as team champion by herself, Paul J. Weber, Sports News, June 7, 2009

Richardson wins state team title alone, Rivals High (from Yahoo Sports), May 12, 2008.

Rochelle, Texas – Wikipedia, http://en.wikipedia.org/wiki/Rochelle,_Texas

Chapter 26: A Perfect Shame

In 1959 Harvey Haddix pitched perhaps the best game ever – and lost, Bob Dvorchak, *Pittsburgh Post-Gazette,* May 24, 2009

Pittsburgh Pirates' Harvey Haddix's 12 Perfect Innings, http://bleacherreport.com/articles/182048-harvey-haddix-perfect-for-12-innings

Harvey Haddix Perfect Game Box Score, http://www.baseball-almanac.com/boxscore/05261959.shtml

Portland songwriter pens ode to the perfect game that got away, Margie Boule, *The Oregonian*, May 24, 2009.

Chapter 27: The Fiesta Fake Out

Keanon Lowe fakes injury to get Dane Ebanez BCS playing time, Matt Walks, *The Daily Emerald*, January 9, 2013.

A Fiesta Bowl story worth rooting for, John Canzano, *The Oregonian*, December 31, 2012

Chapter 28: One For Dad

Team delivers touching moment, Chantel Jennings, *WolverineNation*, October 30, 2012.

Chapter 29: Harvard Beats Yale 29-29

Harvard Beats Yale 29-29, Documentary Film, Kevin Rafferty, 2008

Chapter 30: Responsible Winning

Academy basketball coach sees a win in 100-0 loss, Barry Horn, The Dallas Morning News, January 23, 2009

Chapter 31: Heroic Assistance

Central Washington offers the ultimate act of sportsmanship, Graham Hays,, ESPN.com, April 28, 2008

http://www.wildcatsports.com/news/2008/6/5/3742667.aspx?path=softball

http://www.wildcatsports.com/newa/2008/7/20/4045944.aspx?path=softball

Chapter 32: Winning By Taking Second

Heartwarming proof that sportsmanship is not dead, Michael Katz, *USA Today Sports Online*, January 19, 2013

Chapter 33: Find Your Greatness

Personal Observation

Chapter 34: The 3:59.4 Lesson

The Perfect Mile: Three Athletes, One Goal, and Less Than Four Minutes To Achieve It, Neal Bascomb, 2004, Houghton Mifflin Company.

Chapter 35: Hanging On By A Finger

He Cut Off A Finger – On Purpose, Vickie Bane, *People*, November 3, 2008

Chapter 36: A Perfect Mistake

First 28-out perfect game?, Ben Walker, *Winnipeg Free Press*, June 5, 2010.

Boxscore: Cleveland vs. Detroit - June 2, 2010". *MLB.com*.

http://en.wikipedia.org/wiki/Armando_Galarraga's_near-perfect_game

Chapter 37: The "Around The World" Walk-On

At 43, Navy vet becomes freshman forward, Doug Williams, http://espn.go.com/blog/, January 15, 2013

43-year-old Brian Rice plays basketball for Geneva College, Steve DelVecchio, *Larry Brown Sports*, December 6, 2012

Age is just a number; Navy veteran goes back to school to get a degree and play ball, Amy Farnum, NCAA.com, December 22, 2012

https://www.geneva.edu/page/mbball

Insight of the Day, Bob Proctor, http://www.bobproctormatrix.com, July 24, 2009

The Raymond Aaron Group, http://aaron.com

Chapter 38: The Slowest Runner In America

Worth The Wait, Rick Reilly, *SI Vault*, October 20, 2003

Start With Why: How Great Leaders Inspire Everyone To Take Action, Simon Sinek, Penguin Group Publishing, page 222-4.

Chapter 39: A Rookie Back-Up

Givens up nothing: Hancock goalie saves 43 in upset of Fond du Lac, Brandon Veale, *The Daily Mining Gazette*, January 14, 2013

Chapter 40: What's In A Name

Bo: Life, laughs, and lessons of a college football legend, Bo Schembechler & Mitch Albom, Warner Books, 1989

Chapter 41: The Drought

http://www.thesciac.org

Not exactly on the bubble, Rick Reilly, *ESPN.com*, March 1, 2011

Questions with Bob Sansevere: Caltech guard Ryan Elmquist, a Woodbery High School graduate, Bob Sansevere, *Pioneer Press*, March 1, 2011

Stephen M. Hinkel, Sports Information Director, California Institute of Technology

Chapter 42: We Are One

A Civil War: Army vs. Navy ... A Year Inside College Football's Purest Rivalry, John Feinstein, 1996, Little Brown & Company

CPSIA information can be obtained at www.ICGtesting.com
Printed in the USA
BVOW01s1013220414

351018BV00001B/3/P